AN HISTORICAL
ALMANAC
OF CANADA

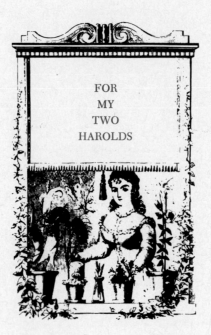

FOR
MY
TWO
HAROLDS

AN HISTORICAL ALMANAC OF CANADA

Being
a Correct and Impartial Account
of
Many Occurences Within
This Dominion
to which is added
a Variety of Useful & Curious Matter
on Such Diverse Subjects
as
Fashions, Manners & Morals
Recipes & Remedies

edited by

LENA NEWMAN

McCLELLAND AND STEWART LIMITED

The Canadian Publishers
McCLELLAND AND STEWART LIMITED
25 Hollinger Road, Toronto 16

DESIGN: Steve Lanik
PRINTED AND BOUND IN CANADA

ACKNOWLEDGEMENTS

Many individuals and institutions have helped me by providing material and suggestions for this book. I am grateful for the help I received from the archives, art galleries, museums, private collectors of Canadiana, libraries, and government agencies in all provinces, the Yukon, and the Northwest Territories. For allowing me access to documents, letters, newspapers, magazines, maps, illustrations, and other items of Canadiana, I must record my special appreciation to the following: the Public Archives of Canada, the National Library, the Canadian Library Association, the National Museum and the National Gallery, the Royal Ontario Museum, the Château de Ramezay, Salle Gagnon de la Bibliothèque de la Ville de Montréal, La Bibliothèque Saint Sulpice, La Bibliothèque de l'Universite de Montréal, the Fraser-Hickson Institute, the Municipal Archives, the Lawrence Lande Foundation for Canadian Historical Research at McGill University, the McGill University Library, Notre Dame de Grace Library for Boys and Girls, Westmount Public Library, and the Montreal Children's Library.

The illustrations used to divide the seasons are courtesy of the National Archives of Canada.

PREFACE

In this Almanac many interesting and out-of-the-way facts about the early years in this vast and wonderful country are assembled for your enjoyment. Here the reader will find the records of the seasons, the folk lore, the anecdotes and sayings, the festivals, and other facts both useful and entertaining. If the stories you read here are familiar to you, so much the better. I hope, for example, that "Old Timothy" will repeat what your grandfather used to say. This almanac includes fragments of poetry and stories long forgotten.

My main concern, however, has been to illustrate the lives of those who came before us – Eskimos, Indians, explorers, voyageurs, fur-traders, sourdoughs, miners, whalers, seal-hunters, ranchers, fishermen – the pioneers of this blessed land. This Almanac takes you through the months and into the lives of these people. We begin on the first day of the calendar, as the settlers did, by exchanging greetings. For although our history tells of conflict and war, it also tells of friendship, loyalty, and understanding. Wherever the settlers met, they exchanged greetings, whether the language was English, French, Indian or Eskimo.

"Happy New Year!"

"Bonne et Heureuse Année! Le Paradis à la fin de vos jours!"

"Sekon! Oserase!"

"Inunnut Tamainnut Quviasuvvimmi Quviasuguva Ssi Arraagunilu Nutaami."

Many friends have contributed anecdotes. One friend, for example, told me of a granduncle from Nova Scotia who, when his mother died in child-birth, dedicated his life to medicine. He studied with the famous Dr. Osler and, what is more, finished ahead of him in the examinations. Then, like Somerset Maugham, he set off to see the world as a ship's doctor. In Hawaii he answered an urgent call from the Queen of the Islands who was desperately ill. The Nova Scotia doctor saved the Queen's life and remained at her court for a year. A lovely story. Checking revealed, however, that the doctor had not attended classes with Osler, but had been his pupil. The piece about the Queen of Hawaii was sheer myth. My friend was quite annoyed with my investigation. He preferred the old story. And, as a matter of fact, so do I. It was Bob Edwards who said, "Some men spoil a good story by sticking to the facts."

The Almanac provides no footnotes. This is intentional because this Almanac is not meant to take the place of history books, biographies or encyclopaedias, but rather to send the reader to such books with greater insight.

How is it possible for me to thank all those who have helped by providing material? In preparing a work such as this, one studies as many of the records and sources as time and energy will allow. One borrows freely, and in the words of Stephen Leacock, "We all acknowledge our debt only to leave it unpaid and borrow more."

My hope is that the reader will find enjoyment in these diverse glimpses into our past.

Montreal, 1967   LENA NEWMAN

WINTER

JANUARY

Almanacs, with their rich and attractive storehouse of miscellany, have been exceedingly popular since antiquity. The British Museum has an Egyptian one three thousand years old, with fortunate days in black, and unlucky ones in red, reversing our custom.

Our Dominion has had its almanacs, albeit not too many. The Dalhousie University Library treasures the first Canadian almanac, the Nova Scotia Calendar, dated 1770, Halifax. Seven years later, Fleury Mesplet, pioneer printer of Montreal, brought out the first of his many almanacs. 1780 saw one by 'Metonicus' also of Halifax and the Québec Almanach, by William Brown, of Quebec City. Others flourished.

It seems time for us to enjoy another of these curious volumes. The years of our history offer exciting substance for an almanac of today.

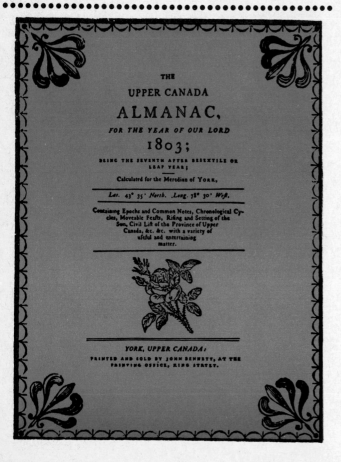

THE
UPPER CANADA
ALMANAC,
FOR THE YEAR OF OUR LORD
1803;
BEING THE SEVENTH AFTER BISSEXTILE OR
LEAP YEAR;
Calculated for the Meridian of York.

Lat. 43° 35' North. Long. 78° 30' West.

Containing Epochs and Common Notes, Chronological Cycles, Moveable Feasts, Rising and Setting of the Sun, Civil List of the Province of Upper Canada, &c. &c. with a variety of useful and entertaining matter.

YORK, UPPER CANADA:
PRINTED AND SOLD BY JOHN BENNETT, AT THE
PRINTING OFFICE, KING STREET.

OUR GRASS ROOTS

Citizens of Toronto are to select a Mayor, Aldermen and Councilmen. More attention should be paid this duty than is usual. Many refrain from the polls... You cannot get Solons and Lycurgeses in a City Council. You must take the best man... and work upward. The candidate for whom you vote may not be perfection... but shortcomings will be corrected by the influence of public opinion.

'Daily Globe' Toronto, Canada West, Jan. 2, 1864.

DID YOU KNOW THAT

Inspired by Dr. W. Grenfell, of the medical missions in Labrador and Newfoundland, there was an active peace corps of 'Wops' and 'Wopesses' (Workers Without Pay) at the beginning of the century. Young people from all stations in life, some at great sacrifice, who could have earned $5 a day, (good money in those days), volunteered to help the 'Labrador Doctor' without pay. They worked in hospitals, schools, boats, kitchens, construction, ditches, or wood cutting. Many well established doctors, surgeons and nurses heeded his call 'to come and help' and spent their vacations, or longer, lending their skills.

A GOLD-HEADED CANE

After the annual freeze-up of the St. Lawrence River, when the first sailing ships arrived at the Port of Montreal, back in the 1830's, the ship's master was honoured with a tall silk hat. The 'Great Britain' docked on April 30, 1840, but later anchorings were noted on May 20, 1854.

Changes have come. For almost a century a gold-headed Malacca cane had replaced the coveted hat. And the timing is different. Ships have been arriving in January. In the early hours of 1966, the Russian freighter 'Indigirka' beat the Danish 'Thora Dan' by minutes, and in the first days of 1967 Capt. Kjell Salbuvik took the Cape Race route full speed ahead to come in three hours before the Danish 'Fenja Dan.'

DATES OF INTEREST

Jan. 2, 1727
General James Wolfe, the hero of Quebec, was born at Westerham, Kent, England.

Jan. 2, 1832
William Lyon Mackenzie presented with a gold medal, worth 60 pounds by his York constituents 'as a token of their appreciation of his political career.'

Jan. 2, 1884
Thirty-one lives lost in Grand Trunk Railway collision at Humber, near Toronto.

Jan. 2, 1908
Canadian coins first struck at the Ottawa Branch of the Royal Mint, England, by His Excellency, The Governor General, Earl Grey. In 1931 the name was changed to the Royal Canadian Mint.

To turn red hair black
Take a pint of the liquor of pickled herrings, half a pound of lamp black, and two ounces of the rust of iron. Mix and boil for twenty minutes. Strain and rub the liquid well into the roots of the hair.

When Canada was beginning to be settled, there were no roads. People travelled by river and the mighty St. Lawrence was called 'the Road of God' ('Le Chemin du Bon Dieu').

Come hither, come hither, my little dog Ponto,
Let's trot down and see where Little York's gone to;
For forty big Tories, assembled in junta,
Have murdered poor Little York in the City of Toronto.'

William Lyon Mackenzie was first Mayor of Toronto, when the name was changed from York to Toronto, 1834.

JANUARY

DATES OF INTEREST

Jan. 1674
François Perrot, Governor of Montreal, and Abbé Fenelon walked on snowshoes from Montreal to Quebec.

Jan. 1832
Montreal, until now an out-port of Quebec, is incorporated and became a port of entry, although a thousand miles from the sea.

The average young lady of the 1800's wondered how many New Year's calls she would receive; the average young man puzzled how to make the greatest number in the shortest time.

Everybody headed home for the paternal blessing on New Year's Day, for all felt this benediction brought good luck in coming ventures. After the immediate family, it was a 'must' to call on other relatives, old friends and associates. This friendly custom of the early 1600's in New France was strengthened by the Scotch settlers of the middle 1700's, who had celebrated this same way in the old country. Calls were spiced with a little frivolity, a little wine, a little flirting.

It is hard to credit this, but one reads that the voyageurs engaged in the Northwest fur trade lived at one time solely upon a quart of maize and one ounce of fat per day during a trip lasting about 14 months. The change to pemmican sounds more like it.

'There is only one class on the plains, and that is the working class. Here and there you meet a gentleman of leisure, but he is called a tramp'.
Howard A. Kennedy, 'New Canada', 1907.

OUR GRASS ROOTS

The Governor-General's Levee-1880

His Excellency, The Governor-General, the Marquis of Lorne, K.T., G.C.M.G., received 400 callers of all classes on New Year's Day, 1880. Sir John A. Macdonald, Sir Charles Tupper, Sir Leonard Tilley, Hon. J. C. Pope, Hon. John O'Connor and Hon. Mr. Baby formed a line immediately in the rear of His Excellency. **(An ancient tradition excluded women.)**
Ottawa 'Daily Citizen' Jan.1, 1880.

There are many stories about the excitability of William Lyon Mackenzie, politician, rebel, journalist, publisher of the 'Colonial Advocate' and the first Mayor of Toronto. Rt. Hon. William Lyon Mackenzie King was his grandson. Of W. L. M. we are told.

'That Mackenzie was the craziest man... wore a wig, and when he got excited — he was always excited... would throw it on the floor... or at you if he felt extra pleasant. You've heard of the time he was brought home with cheering and torches and great doings, and given the gold chain? (Jan. 2, 1832)... He was very pleased and worked up.... Quick as lightning threw the chain at me and the wig on the floor, and then he flung his arms around his mother's neck and kissed her.

The month of January was named for Janus, one of the most honoured of the Roman Gods. As he had two faces, he was able to preside over the New Year very capably, being in a position to look back to the year ending, and forward to the one just commencing.

Carnations, the flowers for January, signify ardent love and betrothal.

'Prince Edward Island Calendar of 1857'
'Corsets were invented by a cruel butcher as a punishment for his wife. She was very loquacious... he put stays on her to take away her breath and prevent her talking. This was inflicted by other heartless husbands. Ladies, in their defence, made a fashion of it.'

'The Moccasin' was what they called the first Grand Trunk Railway train that ran between Montreal and Brockville, Ontario, beginning in the fall of 1855 and continuing for a full century. The Indians, who travelled free, were on it all the time, east in the morning, west at night.

JANUARY

DID YOU KNOW THAT

The French Canadian expression 'It's two or three pipes away' comes from the fact that during a walk of ¾ mile, the pioneer would smoke a pipe of tobacco.

The voyageurs counted the distance in somewhat the same fashion, saying 'It's a twenty pipe trip'. The steersman would cry 'Pipes' and all paddling ceased while the men had a three minute smoke, on the average of every two miles.

To the officers of the police-gentlemen:
I never go up St. John's St., but I am fever-struck. Surely no man in his right senses, unless he be a frenchman, would think of placing the figure of General Wolfe in a situation to point and look at the Falls. In the name of sensibility, gentlemen, endeavour to prevail on the owner to take it down, and if possible place it in a niche in an opposite angle. Contrive to make the General face the right, when he will have the heights in view where he immortalized his name. Consistency.

'Quebec Gazette', Jan. 13, 1785

OLD TIMOTHY

'bout 50 years ago, folks 'round here called a buggy 'a wife-getter'.

The Bell Homestead.   *Bell Telephone Company of Canada.*

The Bell Homestead, as it was when the inventor visited it in 1906 with his eldest daughter Elsie. It was in this year that the Bell Telephone Memorial Society was formed, under Royal patronage and with W. F. Cockshutt, M.P. as President, and in 1909 it bought this property and presented it to the city to be preserved as an historic site.

Drunkard's Soup.
3 or 4 slices of stale bread
¼ lb. lard
5 onions
1 quart water
1 soup spoon of salt herbs.
Cut the bread into small pieces. Place in pot with the lard and onions, finely minced. Brown for some minutes. Add the herbs, pepper and water. Cook slowly for one hour.

'Edmonton is as big as Chicago, but it isn't all built up yet.' Anonymous twentieth century reply to an American who asked the size of the city.

OUR GRASS ROOTS

Legends of the west, always include stories of the old Macleod Hotel, Macleod, Alberta, held by many to be the outstanding hostelry on the continent. These very strict hotel rules were laid down in the early 1880's by Kamoose (Indian for thief) Taylor, the proprietor.

Boots and spurs must be removed at night before retiring.

Every known fluid (water excepted) for sale at bar. Special rates to gospel grinders, and the gambling profession.

Everything cash in advance.
(Tariff-subject to change)

Board $25 per month. Breakfast and dinner – guests must rustle lunch.

Board and lodging $50 per month with wooden bench to sleep on.

Board and lodging $60 per month with bed to sleep on.

Assaults on the cook are strictly prohibited.

Towels changed weekly. Insect powder for sale at the bar.

Pioneer Notes of New France.

Breakfast frequently consisted of bread crusts moistened in cognac.

The dog and cart were commonly used in place of the horse and buggy during all seasons of the year.

In 1645 in Quebec, bread was 15 sols per loaf, (about 25 cents) and a cord of wood 10 sols (about 17 cents).

'The biggest things are always the easiest to do, because there is no competition.'

Sir William Van Horne.

The Indians called January 'The Snow Moon' and also 'Kisapowatu'kinu – moowepesim' or 'The Frost – Exploding – Trees – Moon'.

JANUARY

OUR GRASS ROOTS

Patrick Mackeller's name is not in our history books, but he was the famous intelligence officer who brought valuable knowledge to General Wolfe, prior to the Capture of Quebec. Disguised as a Frenchman, Mackellar was a trusted guest of the Governor and his army staff at the Chateau St. Louis, Quebec, and amassed a great deal of pertinent information.

Using the time-old ruse, he left a dummy sitting in his room, escaped to the waterfront, and swam across to Levis.

When Wolfe arrived at Quebec, Mackellar, as one of his engineers, was able to point out the little path up the cliffs that the British stormed so successfully. The rest is history.

That phenomonon – the Chinook, noted by Sir Alexander Mackenzie, explorer and fur-trader, Jan. 5, 1793.

'Very cold; wind from the South-West, a thaw. At Athabasca, this wind never failed to bring mild weather; when it blew from the opposite quarter, it produced snow. Here, if it blows hard South-West for four hours a thaw is the consequence; if the wind is at North-East it brings sleet and snow. These warm winds come off the Pacific, which cannot be very far, and although they pass over mountains covered with snow, there is not time to cool.'

A New York journal remarks that as Governor-General of Canada, the Marquis of Lorne is quite as acceptable to the United States as anyone else. This is cool. We were not aware that it concerned our neighbours...

'Ottawa Daily Citizen', Jan. 7, 1882

TRIBUTE TO A GREAT CANADIAN.

On January 11, we mark the birthday of Canada's Father of Confederation, Sir John A. Macdonald. Born in 1815, he became Prime Minister in 1867 and with the exception of five years, held that high office until his death in 1891.

⚜ ⚜ ⚜ ⚜ ⚜ ⚜ ⚜ ⚜ ⚜ ⚜ ⚜ ⚜ ⚜ ⚜ ⚜

'Shall brothers be for a' that'.

'Braw fine whusky-suppin' Hieland men' gather in all parts of Canada to-day to do homage to the plowman poet, Robert Burns, who was born over 200 years ago on Jan 25, 1759 near Ayr, Scotland.

In traditional manner, the recollection of 'Wee Rabbie', the famous humanitarian, is marked on Burns night with a toast to 'The Immortal Memory', the music of the bagpipes, exhibitions of Highland dancing and the ceremonial entry of the haggis, carried shoulder high, as the bard's 'To a Haggis' is declaimed.

Fair fa' your honest sonsie face,
Great chieftain o' the puddin' race!
Aboon them a' ye tak your place,
Painch, tripe or thairm:
Weel are ye worthy o' a grace
As lang's my arm.

Burns was born during the 1746-1782 years when the Act of Proscription forbade the wearing of Highland dress in Scotland. Scottish settlers in Canada were however always free to wear Gaelic garb and their pipes resounded in our forests.

*Gentle patrons here I come —
You're mine — I'D be your debtor;
I love you well the whole year round
(And never failed your praise to sound,
So e'er I further outward roam
Just quietly hand out I pray)
And grant me but this single day,
To love your money better.*

This appeared at the top of The Carrier Boy's Address on the first page of the **Ottawa Advocate** on Jan. 1, 1849. In the newspaper tradition of the 1800's, the first issue of the year eulogized the delivery lads in many, many verses, often with political overtones.

JANUARY

The Queen, whose death we have the painful task of communicating to our readers this day, married George the Third, Sept. 7, 1761, and died at the age of 74. As the mother of fifteen children (it may be hoped a race of Kings) she has discharged the important duties of a parent and consort with lustre. Many thought this illustrious female took too active and decided a part in some proceedings a few years ago. They were intimately connected with her family, and the stay of a nation's hopes. On this point we forbear to enlarge. 'Nil nisi bonum de mortuis'.

'Montreal Herald,' Jan. 9, 1819.

The brain drain.

Canadian Patriot Calixa Lavallée died in Boston on Jan. 23, 1891, an American citizen acknowledged as one of the fathers of American music. Born in Verchères, Quebec, his great musical gifts received little encouragement, in Canada, although in his thirties he wrote the music for **'O Canada'**. Fittingly the first home of the Montreal Symphony Orchestra was on the street named for him, but few ever visit his grave in Cote Des Neiges Cemetery, Montreal.

Snowshoe Race, Montreal

OLD TIMOTHY

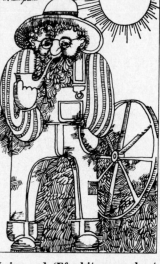

Injun sed, 'Ef white man cheat Injun onct, shame on white man. Ef white man cheat injun twict, shame on Injun'.

DATES OF INTEREST

Jan. 1890
'La Grippe' prevails in Canada as in Europe and the U.S.

Jan. 7, 1867
Timothy O'Hea, a soldier, was given the only Victoria Cross ever awarded for a brave deed not done in the actual presence of an enemy or ever given for service within Canada. In 1866, during the Fenian troubles, O'Hea was guarding a Grand Trunk train of 800 immigrants. He noticed a fire in the consignment of 95 barrels of gunpowder for the Lake Erie front. At great risk, he put out the blaze.

DATES OF INTEREST

Jan. 16, 1813
This is from the very first issue of the 'Acadian Recorder', Halifax, Jan. 16, 1813. Editor and publisher Anthony Henry Holland. The whole of the first edition was reprinted on Jan. 16, 1888, to mark the 75th anniversary. Blackader Bros., publishers, 98 Granville St., Halifax.

An attempt was made to set fire to the Ordinance Store. A quantity of gunpowder and combustibles with a lighted match were providently discovered in a cellar. We trust it will be unnecessary to recommend vigilance to the inhabitants. Jan. 16, 1813.

'An addition to our party now is a Mr. McMurray, who has been twelve days travelling on snowshoes to get here for this holiday, for there he is quite alone . . . The population of the Fort numbers 55. I do not think this country will ever differ much.'

So wrote John Henry Lefroy, the soldier-surveyor of the North-West from Fort Chipewyan, Lake Athabaska, Jan. 1, 1844.

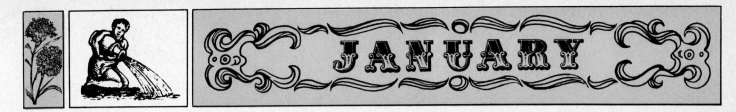

JANUARY

He'll write again.

Mr. Gray, Editor ... Removed from the frivolity of the dandy or the moroseness of the cynic, I admire public amusements and can spend an hour or two at an assembly, country party or concert with satisfaction. Managers of the theatre are complaining loudly that they do not meet with support. If it be from misconduct on their part, they are rightly served; but if the evil is from another source, we must remove it. You shall hear again from ... Yours, O.P. *'Montreal Herald', Jan. 23, 1819.*

DID YOU KNOW THAT

The 'mangeurs du lard', the pork eaters, an integral part of the fur trade, came together for the spring break-up at Lachine, near Montreal, ready to start on the Grand Portage. Of the hard life, full of danger and with little enough financial reward, a 70 year old voyageur at Lake Winnipeg, in 1825 said, 'I have been 42 years in this country, 24 as a light canoe man. No portage was too long. Fifty songs a day were nothing to me. I could carry, paddle, walk and sing with any man I ever saw. No water, no weather stopped paddle or song. I had 12 wives, 50 horses and 6 running dogs, trimmed in the first style. No Bourgeois had better dressed wives than I; no Indian chief finer horses. I wanted for nothing. I spent all for pleasure ... I have not a spare shirt, but there is no life so happy.'

The Hon. M. de Boucherville understood perfectly the aim of the clergy in bringing some religious community here every year, when again and again he opposed in the House the granting of acts of incorporation to these communities. He realized how dangerous to the cause of liberty the accumulation of property in the hands of the clergy is, and his is the merit of having uttered the first warning in Parliament.

Niagara Falls ran dry in the winter of 1848. This was the result of an ice jam in Lake Erie that cut off the water supply of the Niagara River for more than 24 hours.

An Indian in the N.W.T. said in the 1800's, 'When the government made a treaty with us, we were promised doctors and policemen. But we were sent only missionaries.'

The North-West Mounted Police were, in 1884, 'a splendid body of men with a fine contempt for civilians.' Lance-Corporal William Donkin, of the N.W.M.P.

OUR GRASS ROOTS

The Rt. Hon. William Lyon Mackenzie King (Liberal) was in office as Prime Minister of Canada, for the longest period of twenty-one years and five months, serving in three separate terms. The Hon. Sir Charles Tupper (Conservative) held the position for the shortest time of two months and one week. To the Liberal leader the Rt. Hon. Sir Wilfrid Laurier goes the record for serving as Prime Minister for the longest consecutive period of fifteen years and three months. *'L'Avenir', Jan. 18, 1850.*

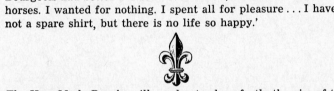

Ice Bridge at Niagara. circa 1880.

OUR GRASS ROOTS

A Serpent of Fire

On Jan. 15, 1873, a fine muster of over 200 snowshoers in a torchlight procession formed a 'serpent of fire' from the gate of McGill College to the top of Mount Royal, in Montreal. At the cry 'Forward', two by two the clubs moved. The 'Toronto Globe' wrote, 'Slowly, silently, like the snow flakes, with the peculiar roll of the shoulders and the jogging of the hips, on went the athletes, in their picturesque costumes, their bright turbans, their fleecy bashilicks (sic) and cerulean tuques.' The Governor-General and Lady Dufferin, in a sleigh, encouraged the clubs which included the Montreal, Alexandra, Maple Leaf, Grand Trunk, Canada, and Victoria. The snowshoers' song 'Tramp, Tramp' was heard on the route and later at the supper party.

Forty names, headed by Simon M'Tavish, sign a notice denouncing the 'felonious practice of stealing horses and horned cattle' and noting that Ephriam Barnes is a notorious offender. $200 reward. *'Montreal Gazette', Jan. 25, 1796.*

Questions that have grown out of the recent session at Ottawa, 'at the first Parliament of the Dominion...' have been pretty freely discussed... the 'Tariff, North West Territory, Stamp Act, Postage on Newspapers' etc., etc.... Now... turn to matters and things nearer home. In a few days our local Legislature will be convened at Fredericton... A large proportion of our members are new men, fresh from the people, and not a few of them are young men... We hear of a new 'School Law', a 'Homestead Law' adapted to the wants of N.B. These measures are in the hands of energetic men. We shall hear from them.
'The Union Advocate', Newcastle, Miramichi, N. B. Jan. 30, 1868.

NICK NAMES
Grey Owl
George Stansfeld, Belaney, writer, lecturer, conservationist of wild life in Canada.

To get away from the dreadful potato famine in Ireland, 100,000 Irish immigrants came to Canada in 1847.

DID YOU KNOW THAT

With handsome, fast ponies easily available, polo became a 'must' in the N.W.T., in 1884-5. The Polo Magazine of January 1897, wrote 'broom handles and cricket balls were used.' (Were the latter brought out by the English remittance men?) Clubs from Calgary, High River and Macleod played in 1892, and from then on the game flourished.

An Australian poet, A. B. (Banjo) Paterson, christened the formidable Pekisko, High River, Polo Club of 1904, the 'Geebungs' and wrote: –

'They were long and wiry natives from the rugged mountainside,
And the horse was never saddled that the Geebungs couldn't ride.
But their style of playing polo was irregular and rash,
They had mighty little science, but a mighty lot of dash,
And they played on mountain ponies that were muscular and strong,
Though their coats were quite unpolished, and their manes and tails were long.
And the game was so terrific that 'ere half the time was gone,
A spectator's leg was broken – just from merely looking on.'

The Death of General Wolfe.

Poetry in Canada is at a discount. Epic, dramatic, lyric, spasmodic, it is a drug, a very assafetida pill in the literary market. The publishers keep it at arm's length; the public turns up its nose at it. It is even worse than worthless. Poetry does not grow in Canada.
'Canadian Illustrated News', Jan. 20, 1872.

DID YOU KNOW THAT

'Necessity is...'

Oddly enough it was because Louis Hébert needed herbs for his medicines that be became the first Canadian farmer. Coming to Acadia, in 1604, he helped sick settlers with the same remedies he had used in France, where he was an apothecary at the Court, as well as an attorney. Ten years farming at Port Royal was enough for him, and he returned to France. But his friend, Champlain, coaxed him back to Quebec City, where he farmed in Upper Town. Champlain called him 'the first head of a family, residing in the country, to live on what he grows.' Outside the City Hall in Quebec, he is shown on a monument, holding up a sheaf of the first wheat he had grown in Canada. Perhaps he shares honours with Guillaume Couillard, also called 'the first tiller of the soil,' who lived in Quebec at about the same time and married one of Hébert's daughters.

Many French Canadians trace their ancestry to this Louis Hébert who died in 1627, as the result of a fall.

'The Poet of the Yukon', 'The Bard of the North', and 'The Canadian Kipling' was how the world knew Robert William Service.

Born in Preston, England, on Jan. 16, 1874, he was taken to Scotland where he tried to conform to the family banking interests. But the call of adventure took him to Canada in 1894 – in his pocket, the traditional $5 bill, and the optimism of the twenty-year old.

Years up and down the Pacific Coast included work with the Canadian Bank of Commerce in Vancouver, Victoria, Kamloops, Whitehorse and Dawson. But poetry was his love. His first volume of verse 'Songs of a Sourdough' 1907, also called 'The Spell of the Yukon' was an immediate success. In addition to many popular collections of poems, he wrote 6 novels, which were less favourably received. His cabin-in-the woods at Dawson still stands as when he wrote 'It's the stillness that fills me with peace.'

JANUARY

In the most inexcusable blunders which Canada has perpetrated in her attempted acquisition of this Territory . . . is that of accepting as the true sentiments of this people, those uttered by the quondam Canadian party which laid the foundations of our present trouble . . . Any other government . . . would have thought . . . of delegating some agent to enquire into the sentiments . . . of a people whom they expected to rule, but to them it appears it never occurred.

'The New Nation', Winnipeg, Jan. 21, 1870.

The Baby's Cradle.

OUR GRASS ROOTS

Thomas Tremlett, who had the distinction of holding the office of Chief Justice for two provinces – Newfoundland, 1803-13; and Prince Edward Island, 1813-24, was untrained in the law, and of a tactless and impatient nature. The Governor of Newfoundland was petitioned to remove him from office, on three specific charges. Tremlett replied, 'To the first charge, your Excellency, I answer that it is a lie, to the second charge, I say that it is a damned lie, and to the third charge, It is a damned infernal lie, and, your Excellency, I have no more to say.'

As it happened Prince Edward Island was having a turbulent time with the equally fiery Chief Justice Ceasar Colclough. With wisdom and tact the two provinces exchanged their Chief Justices.

Peter M. Choice respectfully informs that he will take profiles in the Museum at the house of Mr. Pierson, Old Market Place, where he has a Grand Machine for that purpose. He will also paint the profiles as natural as life. Cutting only, 15d.; for those who call to see the museum – half price.

'The Montreal Herald', Jan. 27, 1816.

The 'Drum', believed to be the first newspaper of its kind in the Canadian Arctic was issued on Jan. 6, 1966 as a six-page duplicated production in English, Eskimo and Loucheux Indian dialect. Stories in Slavey dialect will be added. The publisher is Tom Butters, graduate of the School of Journalism, Carleton University, and formerly regional administrator at Inuvik for the Department of Northern Affairs. Distribution in Inuvik, a community of 2,300 people, 200 miles inside the Arctic Circle, is by carrier. Under 'Subscription rates', one reads – 'Since many subscribers may live in the 'bush', subscriptions may be paid in either cash or kind.'

DATES OF INTEREST

Jan. 30, 1646
Father Anne de Nouë left Three Rivers to go to Fort Richelieu, but losing his way, perished in the snow.

Jan. 30, 1649
On this date, 'there were in the Huron country and its vicinity, 18 Jesuit priests, 4 lay brothers, 23 men serving without pay, 7 hired men, 4 boys and 8 soldiers.'

Jan. 30, 1815
Bishop Strachan, of York, wrote his famous letter to Thos. Jefferson, Former President of the United States.

Jan. 31, 1809
Jurist Lemuel Allen Wilmot was born in Sunbury County, N.B. Entering politics as a Reformer, he became Lieut.-Gov. of New Brunswick in 1868.

Jan. 31, 1825
James Reid named Chief Justice of Montreal court. The name of King's Bench was retained until 1844 when it was provided the name should be Queen's Bench when the sovereign was a Queen, and King's Bench when a King.

Jan. 31, 1839
A compromise was reached in the 'Aroostook War' on the undecided boundaries between New Brunswick and Maine. Lumbermen of both areas were troubled.

Jan. 31, 1863
Sir John Beverley Robinson, Bart., died, at Beverley House, Toronto. Of his appointment as Chief Justice of U.C., it was said 'He had few equals in the history of Canadian judicature'.

'The French Canadian father who today does not have his son learn English, does not do justice to his child, for he forces him to remain behind in the struggle for existence.'
Sir Wilfrid Laurier, House of Commons Debates, 1890.

FEBRUARY

Spinning and Carding

'When a doryman sed 'from anchor to anchor', he meant a feller who duz his part well the whole of the voyage.'

One hundred and twenty-three verses.

A travesty of John Gilpin, dealing with the 'Rebellion Events in the Canadas', and, of course, William Lyon Mackenzie, appeared in the Cobourg Star, Feb. 7, 1838. Only the first three of the one hundred twenty-three verses, by a Miss FitzGibbon, are given here: —

There lived in famed Toronto
  town,
A man not very big,
A belted knight was he
  likewise, –
Knight of the old bay wig.

Mackenzie was this hero called,
From Scotia's land he came,
To sow and reap – if e'er he
  could –
The seeds of future fame.

Well taught was he to broil
  and scold,
To slander and to lie,
The good to libel – but the bad
Around him close to tie.

(About 1908) 'A homesteader paid . . . ten dollars when he filed. This was all . . . that changed hands, and some of the finest land that ever lay outdoors 'as level as the water when the wind don't blow' was acquired in this manner . . . You bet your ten dollars against the government's 160 acres of land that you would not starve to death on it in three years. Not many did, but with drought, hail, rust, sawfly, and frost, most farmers did their share of complaining . . . There was a saying . . . that the homesteader was the only man who could start with nothing, lose money all his life, and die rich'.

From 'West of Yesterday' by George Shepherd.

The name – February.

The month of February takes its name from the Latin 'februare' meaning 'to purify'. It was only in 452 B.C. that it took its present place in the calendar. Before that it was placed at the end of the year, that is, when it was included at all.

'If these sketches should prove the means of deterring one family from sinking their property, and shipwrecking all their hopes, by going to reside in the backwoods of Canada, I shall consider myself amply repaid for revealing the secrets of the prison-house, and feel that I have not toiled and suffered in the wilderness in vain.'

So wrote Susanna Moodie of England who emigrated with her husband in 1832 to settle near Cobourg, Upper Canada, where the family endured the the hardships of pioneer life.

Old-time remedies from the French Canadian habitant.

To cure a horse of colic, set a pint of water in a pan on the stove. As it boils, the horse will improve. When the water has boiled away entirely, and the pan is turned upside down, the horse will be cured.

DID YOU KNOW THAT

There are many stories telling how Canada came by its name. Some say it derives from the Algonquin word 'Cantata', meaning welcome, used by the Indians in greeting Jacques Cartier, when he first reached our shores, at what is now the Gulf of St. Lawrence, in 1534.

Others say it comes from the Iroquois 'Canatha' meaning 'a collection of huts'.

We are told that the Spaniards said 'ACANADA' or 'There is nothing there' to indicate that they did not see the gold they were seeking, as they sailed along the coast of the Gulf of St. Lawrence.

The Portuguese, who were supposed to have sailed up the St. Lawrence River long before Jacques Cartier, saw the waters narrow, as they approached what is now Quebec, and exclaimed 'Canada', meaning 'a narrow passage.'

Somewhat similar is the story concerning the early Basque navigators, to whom the word 'Canada' meant 'a straight or narrow passage'.

The 'Novascotian' of more than a century ago differed with our photographers who have their clients 'make a pretty mouth' by saying 'cheese' or 'Sex'. The 'Novascotian' told its women readers to say 'besom' before entering a room to achieve a bland serene expression; 'brush' for a noble bearing; 'flip' for small pretty lips, and 'Cabbage' to enlarge a smallish mouth.

OUR GRASS ROOTS

The first 2,073 Doukhobors, the largest number of immigrants to cross the Atlantic at one time, arrived at Halifax at 3 p.m. January 20, 1899. By summer, the total 7,427, had spread through the reserves of Saskatchewan bringing vitality to the West. They were welcomed with warmth, and each adult male was given a 160-acre homestead.

Since 1924, it is estimated that the Sons of Freedom have cost Canada's tax-payers a minimum of $20,124,185 in actual destruction and for police and court costs. This figure does not include the thousands of dollars spent to police, shelter and feed those involved in hundreds of demonstrations, nude parades and hunger strikes. *Simma Holt, Terror In the Name of God*

'The post laureate of the Cariboo' is what the miners called young James Anderson who left Scotland in 1863 for the new gold-fields in British Columbia. His rhymes and songs appeared in the 'Cariboo Sentinel', of Barkerville, B.C. in 1865, and shortly after as 'Sawney's Letters', the first pamphlet to be printed in the Cariboo. Weary of 8 years hard luck, he left for England. However, his songs, that the old hands felt recorded their experiences so faithfully, are still heard in the annual Barkerville Review, at the government-restored Theatre Royal. This song is to the air 'Young Man from the Countree' –

The Dancing Girls of Cariboo of 1866

We are dancing girls in Cariboo,
And we're liked by all the men,
In gum boots and a blanket coat –
And e'en the upper ten!
We all of us have swee-eet-hearts,
But the dearest of all to me!
Is that young man who wistfully
Casts those sheep's eyes at me!

The Crown of the House is Godliness.
The Beauty of the House is Order.
The Glory of the House is Hospitality.
The Blessing of the House is Contentment.
Inscription over the fire place of a Lower Canada home.

To keep green vegetables, place on damp stones covered with a damp cloth. Bury parsley in a jar during winter, or dry by hanging in a warm room. Tie onions in bundles and hang from beams. Beet-roots, parsnips, carrots and potatoes are best kept in dry sand all winter. *Hints from Upper Canada, 1875.*

FEBRUARY

'Doctors! Go to the wounded! Do not wait for them to come to you!'

Words of Dr. Henry Norman Bethune, who interrupted his Toronto medical course to enlist in the first contingent of the CEF in 1914, was born in Gravenhurst, Ontario in 1890. The first medical man to bring blood banks to the battlefields, he saved hundreds in Spain in 1936-7 and in China, where he died on Nov. 13, 1939, of septicemia, contracted while operating at the front with inadequate supplies.

'Pau Chu En' (White Seek Grace), the name by which masses of Chinese remember him, is entombed at East Shansi. Bethune International Peace Hospitals and Bethune Medical Schools stretch from Yenan to Peking.

Mrs. Emily Ferguson Murphy, 1868-1933, Judge of the Juvenile Court for the Province of Alberta, wrote under the name of Janey Canuck, conducting a popular daily feature in the 'Edmonton Bulletin' called Janey Canuck's Motto. Some of her sayings follow –

'Lean on no one. Find your own centre and live in it, surrendering it to no person or thing.'

'Avoid like the plague the company of despondent people; pessimism leads to weakness, as optimism leads to power.'

'The commonest and cheapest of all pleasures is conversation, It is the greatest past-time of life.'

OLD TIMOTHY

In the backwoods of Ontario, folks usta say
'Happy is the wooin'
That's not long a-doin'.'

DATES OF INTEREST

Feb. 13, 1641
The Iroquois began war against Canada, still bearing resentment that Champlain created when he sided with the Hurons and the Algonquins. From east to west, the Iroquois were the Mohawks, Oneidas, Onondagas, Cayugas, and the Senecas, and they called their confederacy 'The Long House'.

Feb. 13, 1644
The King of France approved the grant of the Island of Montreal to the Society of Notre-Dame de Montreal.

Feb. 1759
In this year of the conquest, food prices rose. Beef went from 3c a pound to 40c; bacon from 6c to 70c; butter from 5c to 70c; eggs from 3c to 70c a dozen; and chicken from 8c to 60c each.

Salmon Weirs. St John Harbour.

In 1861, the 'New York Herald' threatened Canada with 400,000 disciplined troops, 'who will ask no better occupation than to destroy the last vestiges of British rule on the American continent and annex Canada to the United States.'

Vancouver is called the City of Lights and Flowers.

In New France, at the end of the 17th century, matrimony was not only encouraged but enforced. If a man married before twenty, he was granted fifty livres. Eighteen was the usual age for bridegrooms. The girls became brides at fourteen and fifteen, and received the same bounty as long as they were married by sixteen. These gifts, known as 'The King's Pleasure', were paid on the marriage morn.

'A woman of taste is always an engaging object.'
'Letters of Mephibosheth Stepsure' by Thomas McCulloch, 1821.

DID YOU KNOW THAT

'Nobody was more surprised that I', said Charles Connell, New Brunswick's Postmaster-General, in 1860, when 500,000 five-cent stamps appeared each with his likeness, at a time when only portraits of the Royal Family were used. Public and private rows caused Connell's resignation, although he made amends by paying himself for the substitute stamps which were immediately ordered – with Queen Victoria's portrait. Also, he burned the ill-fated issue of stamps with his picture, on his own front lawn. All that he could find, that is. From time to time, a vertical Connell, catalogued at $2000 or more, turns up, and causes real excitement among philatelists.

Charles Connell lived down the scandal, and became M.P. for Carleton County, N.B. in Canada's first parliament of 1867.

FEBRUARY

How things have changed!

In 1877, it was thought necessary to equip the kitchen of a small family with the following pieces of wooden ware – a wash bench, three sizes of wash tubs, a wash board, a skirt board, a bosom board, a clothes stick, a flour barrel cover, chopping bowls, wood boxes and a clothes wringer.

'Of all the 17 senses, I like common sense about as well as any of 'em.

Justice Thomas Chandler Haliburton, 1840.

In the early 1800's.

'Moonias' was the term given by the Métis and Indians of the Northwest to a greenhorn who had to learn the ways of the area.

'Benjamin Pipe, an Assiniboia farmer, is on the way to England to induce 50 healthy, experienced, good-looking girls to accompany him back to the prairies. The girls will begin as servants at about fifteen dollars a month, but it will be understood that the fault will lie in them, if they do not soon become mistresses of 50 households. Wives, not servants, are what the west needs . . . They tell us that female domestics are almost impossible to get for love or money. The west will give both love and money.'
'Saturday Night', Toronto, 1905.

DID YOU KNOW THAT

In St. Andrews, New Brunswick, the Shiretown Inn Lot was a grant to United Empire Loyalist Thomas Wyer, and was first utilized as a hotel about 1800 by Edward Pheasant. When a gang set fire to the livery stable burning 18 horses and the building, Angus Kennedy re-built on the same site in 1881.

Labourers and carpenters received only 90 cents for a ten-hour day. Soon the bar opened, and any worker who did not spend part of his earnings drinking was fired. The inn became the centre of activity. On election days the proprietor had to reign over the bar with a club in hand lest the visitors from the islands of Grand Manan, Campobello and Deer Island took it upon themselves to partake of free liquor.

In 1670, Jean Baptiste Talon, Intendant of New France, wrote King Louis XIV, of France, and his ministers asking that 'Carefully chosen girls be sent as brides'. A Mademoiselle Etienne was sent from Canada to accompany the girls back, and she was given fifty écus for their comforts. The girls came from Normandy and other parts of France where there was acute poverty. They were between sixteen and forty, for no woman past the age of child-bearing, was to receive the bounty. It is said that they were interviewed by priests, and that nuns made the voyage with them, for if the ocean was rough, so indeed were the seamen.

The amethyst, the birthday gem for February, is said to insure one's husband's love and also to have a 'sobering' effect (in the A.A. sense!). In addition, it denotes perfection. In the New Testament, the amethyst stood for Matthias, who had the gift of tongues and was filled with the desire to please God. This stone is supposed to be happy for everyone. It is frequently found in the Bay of Fundy region of Nova Scotia, in New Brunswick and Ontario.

Alexander Graham Bell. Telephone Historical Collection Bell, Telephone Company.

Alexander Graham Bell invented the telephone in 1874 in Brantford, Ont., at the age of 27. When he was dying (aged 75), cautioned not to hurry his dictation, he replied, 'But I have to. So little time. So much to do.'

OUR GRASS ROOTS

To understand our west, one must know the weather. Only those who have lived with the Chinook, can recreate the legendary 'Johnny Chinook.'

Our lively Johnny is everywhere in Alberta, in legends and tall tales. He is a part of every pioneer like Sir Alexander Mackenzie, Samuel Hearne, David Thompson, Colonel Dan Macleod, of old timers like Twelve Foot Davis, Black John Ware, Kootenai Brown, of characters like Bob Edwards, loveable Hughena McCorquodale, Senator Dan Riley and Old Kamoose, of the Red River carts, the bull whackers, railroad men, Indians, Mounted Police, ranchers, prospectors, con men, Britain's forgotten younger sons, of everyone who helped to build Alberta. There is no end to the stories about Johnny Chinook. And every one is different, each time you hear it.

Their weather? Don't ask about it unless you have lots of time to sit and listen. Albertans rival Paul Bunyan and his 'Year of the Two Winters'. They had two summers in one winter, and no summer at all the next year.

FEBRUARY

DESIGN OF THE CANADIAN FLAG

1. *Technical description*

   A red flag of the proportions two by length and one by width (or 64 units in length and 32 units in width (depth) as shown in the accompanying diagram), containing in its centre a white square the width of the flag, with a single red maple leaf centered therein.

2. *Colours*

   Red (Scarlet)—British Admiralty Colour Code no. T1144 for nylon worsted bunting, and no. T818A for other bunting (These red patterns are used also in the red ensign and in the union jack).

   White—British Admiralty Colour Code no. T1145 for nylon worsted bunting, and no. T819 for other bunting.

The Queen's Printer, Ottawa, has issued this heraldic description of the flag – 'Gules on a Canadian pale argent a maple leaf of the first.' (Gules is the heraldic term for red as 'argent' is for white, shining or silvery).

The Queen's Personal Flag, specifically for use in Canada, comprises the three divisions of the Arms of Canada and Her Majesty's own device in gold on blue, the initial 'E'' surmounted by the St. Edward's Crown within a chaplet of roses.

DATES OF INTEREST

Feb. – 1732
Religious houses were forbidden to shelter fugitives from justice.

Feb. – 1754
The population of Quebec was double that of Montreal – 8,000 as against 4,000.

Feb. 22, 1893
'Lager beer of not more than 4% alcohol is a temperance drink' voted the Legislative Assembly of Quebec.

Feb. 15, 1634
The Hundred Associates granted six arpents of land at Three Rivers to the Jesuits.

Feb. 15, 1881
Letters patent were issued to the Canadian Pacific Railway Company. The Government gave $25,000,000 and 25,000,000 acres of land for building the C.P.R.

Feb. 16, 1857
Flood damage throughout Canada West was general and considerable. The Humber rose, but since the flood of 1850, few dwellings have been exposed, so the damage was chiefly to mill-dams and bridges.

DID YOU KNOW THAT

When our pioneer ancestors spoke of 'bazzle skins' they meant sheepskin tanned with bark. Bombazeen was a twilled dress fabric of silk or cotton with worsted filling. Bombazette was a thin worsted cloth. Bugles were long glass beads for trimming. Dresses were made of cassimere or kerseymere, a soft wool, and overcoats of Fearnought, a very thick, very warm, woollen cloth, which as the name indicates, stood up to any weather change. Sarsnett was a popular soft silk lining.

Alexander Mackenzie, Prime Minister of Canada, 1873-78, was referred to as 'A grand man on his legs.' Sir George Simpson was called 'The King of the Fur Traders'; Philemon Wright, 'The Father of the Ottawa' and the Indians called Métis Cuthbert Grant 'Wappeston' which means 'White Ermine' because of his fair skin and swift movements.

A sixty cent unused 1927 Newfoundland stamp, which marked the Newfoundland-Rome sea-plane flight by Italian Commander de Pinedo, sold for $11,100 recently. An even better price of $16,500 was fetched by a 1933 black Newfoundland airmail stamp, commemorating the transatlantic flight of Italian General Italo Balbo. Through error, this $4.50 stamp had been overprinted on a ten-cent yellow instead of a 75-cent bistre.

Those who could, paid.

In the 1870's Joe Beef's Tavern on Montreal's bustling waterfront catered to tough sea-going men. Those who could, paid; but no one was denied a free lunch and his special five-cent drink. Lodging was ten cents (or free!) with a compulsory morning scrub. Although no church man himself, Joe once fed and lodged 50 down-and-outers and then marched them to a nearby chapel.

Actually an Irishman, Charles McKiernan, Joe earned his nickname for the skill with which he 'attracted' sides of beef, while an artillery sergeant. He had a passion for quantity. Bread loaves were stacked from floor to ceiling, and if a live smelly buffalo and a moth-eaten black bear shared the corner, who cared?

Joe Beef's sign is still to be seen, and to sailors the world over, he is a legend.

'We lead, let those follow who can.'

This was the motto of a four-page newspaper, the 'Leader', which William Maxwell Aitken, Lord Beaverbrook, published in 1893 in Newcastle, N.B., when he was fourteen. It lasted four issues. Twenty-four years later, he bought his first newspaper, the London 'Daily Express'.

FEBRUARY

Postmark 'Love'.

The very old game-song, 'I sent a letter to my love', has warmer sentimental meaning today, for one can mail through the post office at Love, Sask., a village of 132 loveable (no doubt) inhabitants. Unless sweethearts prefer that their tender Valentine missives carry the mark of time-honoured Cupids, the seat of Newfoundland's first formal colony, founded in 1610. Or to send billet doux from Heart's Content (1610-11), Heart's Desire (1720) or Heart's Delight (1780), all close together on Trinity Bay, Nfld. Cupids was really called Cuper's Cove until 1630, when the name was corrupted by usage.

North of the 53rd. parallel.

The trapper, prospector, riverman and bushman – those who built the north with colour and tradition – are honoured each February at the Trapper's Festival at The Pas, in northern Manitoba.

Their Dog Derby, now known as the World's Championship Dog Race, started over a half-century ago with a 150-mile non-stop run in 24 hours, 47 minutes. Mushers and dogs train all winter for this longest dog race in the world, a grueling test of endurance and courage for the dogs who must finish with their sleds; and for the mushers, who run many miles to rest their dogs.

Other Festival events include – the Trappers' Rendez-vous, trap-setting, North Pole climbing, bannock baking, moose calling, ice fishing, an Indian pow-pow, musher's banquet of stew and bannock, and the highly energetic search for the elusive ice-worm.

Samuel de Champlain married Hélène, daughter of Nicholas Boullé, a secretary of the chamber of the King of France, in 1610 when she was said to be but eleven and he well over forty. It was a childless marriage. She spent only the years from 1620 to '24 with him in Canada, and came to be greatly beloved by the small Indian children as well as their parents. They would walk long distances to gaze into the small mirror which she wore suspended by a cord from her neck. They said to one another, 'This beautiful noble lady loves us so much, she carries our picture always on her person.'

The Buckskin Club.   The Public Archives of Canada.

Sir John Alexander Macdonald

AH, John A., John A., how I love you! How I wish I could trust you!

Anon., Liberal member of the Legislature, 1863 to Sir John A. Macdonald, from Cartwright, 'Reminiscences', 1912

EVEN LORD MOUNT STEPHEN DIDN'T WIN THEM ALL!

The story goes that Lord Mount Stephen, of Canadian railway fame, and president of the Bank of Montreal, was in Hamilton in 1876 at a business luncheon with leading financiers. Alexander Graham Bell had requested that they watch a demonstration of something he called a telephone. This they did, agreeing that it was a very clever little toy, but only that.

Cure for Chilblains.

Place red hot coals in a vessel. Throw upon them a handful of corn meal. Hold the feet in the dense smoke, renewing the coals and meal, till the pain is relieved. This has been known to make very marked cures when all other remedies have failed. *Ontario remedy, 1881.*

OUR GRASS ROOTS

For sale, servants for life, a black woman, Peggy, 40, and her son, Jupiter, 15, for $150 and $200. She is a tolerable cook and washerwoman, understands perfectly making soap and candles. Payable in 3 years. One-fourth less for ready money.

York 'Gazette and Oracle', Feb. 19, 1806.

The historic estate, first owned by Louis d'Ailleboust de Coulonge, a founding member of the Compagnie Notre-Dame of Montreal, and the third governor of New France from 1648 to 1651, was originally known as 'Castellany of Coulonge'. It has had several name changes to Powel Place and Spencer Wood, by which it was called for 140 years from 1811 to 1950 taking the name from Spencer Perceval, an English Prime Minister.

Newfoundland is suffering sorely from Tory oppression and she's commencing to kick. Canada will kick on the fifth of March with such force as will hurl John A. and his thieving Conservative gang into a half century's obliviousness and MORE, for Canada will take longer to forget the soreness of the grasp the Tory traitors had on her throat.

Montreal 'Patriot', Feb. 21, 1891.

FEBRUARY

To cure a felon . . . Wrap a piece of rock salt, size of a butternut in a green cabbage leaf, if to be had, if not in wet brown paper. Lay in hot embers, cover as to roast an onion. After 20 minutes, take out and powder as fine as possible. Mix the powder with so much hard soap to make a salve. If the soap has little turpentine (may be known by smell) add a little, but if soap smells pretty strong, none need be added. Apply the salve to the felon. It will, in a few hours (sometimes in a few minutes) destroy the felon, and remove all pain. Never fails.

Quebec 'Mercury', 1807.

It was definitely established today that Sir Frederick Banting, Military Cross, co-discoverer of insulin, William Bird and William Snaithan had been killed in the accident that overtook their plane on the Newfoundland coast.

Montreal 'Star', Feb. 24, 1941.

Dr. Banting was flying to Great Britain on a 'mission of high national and scientific importance' when the plane crashed in attempting a forced landing in a remote region.

OLD TIMOTHY

'Many a homesteader is alive today becuz some prairie farmer kept a light shinin' all night when a blizzard come up. That's a good neighbour.'

DATES OF INTEREST

Feb. 23, 1879
First issue of 'La Patrie', Montreal.

Feb. 23, 1909
J. A. D. McCurdy, later Lieutenant-Governor of Nova Scotia, flew the Silver Dart for one half mile across frozen Baddeck Bay, from Alexander Graham Bell's Aerial Experimental Association base, scoring a major success for the inventor's 'heavier-than-air' machines.

Feb. 29, 1704
De Rouville, with 50 Canadians and 200 Indians, attacked and burned Deerfield and captured John Williams, the minister. In retaliation, Col. Church marched against Acadia, damaging Grand Pré.

The Silver Dart   *The Public Archives of Canada*

DID YOU KNOW THAT

Sir Wilfred Grenfell, the medical missionary, master mariner and writer, who was born in England on Feb. 28, 1865, had the same love of sea adventure as his ancestor Sir Richard Grenville, who defied the Spanish fleet at Azores in 1591. From the age of 24, when he graduated as a doctor, he dedicated himself to Labrador and Newfoundland through the Royal National Mission to Deep Sea Fishermen. He said 'Following Christ has given me more fun and adventure than any other kind of life'. He founded hospitals, nursing stations, orphanage-boarding schools, co-operative stores, industrial and agricultural centres. The fisher-folk loved and trusted him. He told Hudson's Bay Company directors, 'I hold no brief for any company . . . the brief I hold is for the catchers of the fur.' A tough business man said 'If Wilfred Grenfell were to come through that door, I would feel Christ had entered the room.'

Mayonnaise Recipe. 1909.

Sift a pound or two red pepper over two ounces butter, until the mass smokes. Break an egg if you care to, but do not waste it on the mayonnaise. Put it into a long glass, beat with fork, add sugar, a little milk, and a heaping glass of whiskey. Sprinkle nutmeg on top, drain to last drop. After smacking your lips, set the rest of the mayonnaise on the top pantry shelf and leave it there.

It would be an understatement to say that there had been no love lost between Bishop Strachan and Robert Gourlay, in the uneasy years during and after the War of 1812. Gourlay, the would-be reformer and agitator, would have been distasteful to John Strachan anyway, but he gave the Bishop excellent cause for dislike, when he said publicly 'Strachan is a lying little fool of a renegade Presbyterian'.

During the gold rush in British Columbia, in 1860, the miner called for 'Cariboo Turkey' when he wanted bacon, and for 'Cariboo Strawberries' when he felt like ordering beans.

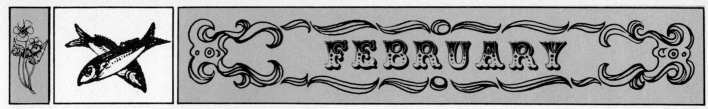

FEBRUARY

DID YOU KNOW THAT

This story is told about Sir Edward Wentworth Beatty, who was president of the Canadian Pacific Railway at a time when many difficult problems seemed to defy solution. On a trip out west, his train stopped near a gang labouring on the tracks. Sir Edward finished his beautifully served breakfast, and stepped down to have a word or two with the men. As he returned to his special car, he inhaled the fresh crisp mountain air, thumped his chest, and said, 'It does a man good to rough it!'

Expressive Newfoundland sayings.

The death of a horse is the life of a crow.

As quick as you'd say 'trapsticks.'

Orillia, Ontario, is known as 'The Sunshine Town' for that is where Stephen Leacock wrote his 'Sunshine Sketches of a Little Town.'

WHEN THE ICE–WORMS NEST AGAIN.

There's a husky, dusky maiden in the arctic
In her igloo, she's waitin' there in vain,
Oh, I guess I'll put my mukluks on and ask her,
If she'll wed me WHEN THE ICE-WORMS NEST AGAIN.

Chorus . . . In the land of the pale blue snow
Where it's ninety-nine below,
And the polar bears are roamin' o'er the plain
In the shadow of the pole
I will clasp her to my soul,
We'll be happy WHEN THE ICE-WORMS NEST AGAIN.

Oh, the weddin' feast will be seal oil and blubber,
In our kayaks we'll roam the boundless main,
How the walruses will turn their necks to rubber,
We'll be happy WHEN THE ICE-WORMS NEST AGAIN.

And when all the blinkin' icebergs bound around us,
She'll present me with a bouncin' baby boy,
All the polar bears will dance a rumba 'round us
And the walruses will click their teeth with joy.

Words and music by Mona Symington, Marion Williamson and Joyce Kolgan.

Eskimo Mother and Child.   The Public Archives of Canada!

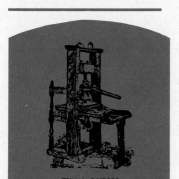

THE NEW AND IMPROVED WASHINGTON PRESS

This newly improved press will make it possible for us to publish a much better newspaper for our increasing number of subscribers, and in which we take great pride.

'The artist is an agitator, a disturber of the peace —quick, impatient, positive, restless and disquieting. He is the creative spirit of life working in the soul of man.'
Dr. Norman Henry Bethune, Ontario–born thoracic surgeon, who was himself a painter, and who pioneered in bringing blood banks to the battlefields.

Letters from the Northwest tell of a custom among the women of the early Forts in the middle 1800's. Those who had suffered the loss of a child, would place a bough over the graves of the little ones, each time they passed.

OUR GRASS ROOTS

Joe Beef's handbills – 1870.

The proprietor of Joe Beef's Tavern believed in advertising. One freely distributed handbill said:

'Joe Beef, of Montreal, the Son of the People,
Cares not for Pope, Priest, Parson or King William of the Boyne;
All Joe wants is the coin.
He trusts in God in summertime to keep him from all harm,
When he sees the first frost and snow, poor Joe
Trusts to the Almighty Dollar and good old maple wood
To keep his belly warm,
For Churches, Chapels, Preachers and such stuff
Montreal has already got enough.'

A bill of fare listed:

Cooked Goose, Turkey, Turtle – 10 cents;
Small fry, 'round the city, only 5 cents.

MARCH

Whereas my wife, Margaret, is inclined to tarry with her friends the winter over, this is to give notice that I shall not pay any debt contracted by her, and to forbid every one to credit her on my account.
Azariah Pritchard
Quebec, 1816

The Indian name for March is the Crow Moon or Mikisewepesim, the Eagle Moon.

St. John . circa . 1880.

To tell the weather ahead, drop cubed sugar in your coffee mug. Bubbles in the centre – fine weather; bubbles sticking to the cup – rainy or snowy days.

It is said that a Hot Cross Bun kept from Good Friday to Good Friday will bring good luck to the household.

Vin du pays

'In some places there are many wild vines loaded with grapes. Some have made wine of them through curiosity. I tasted it and it seemed to me very good.' So wrote Le Jeune in 'Jesuit Relations', 1636. But Indian legends tell of ceremonial wines offered to their gods under the Niagara Falls, long, long before the coming of the white man.

Although there was a small vineyard at Cooksville, Ont., in 1811, George Barnes established the oldest winery at St. Catharines in 1873. 'The use of native wine is growing ... as the use of spirits and malt liquours becomes less pronounced ... a great aid to temperance. (The 'Daily Standard', St. Catharines, March 29, 1894).

Post Office, Quebec, 8th March, 1817

A mail for Ristigouche and Chaleur Bay will be made up and closed at this office on Wednesday morning next, the 12th inst. at eleven o'clock.

Hy Cowan, P.M.

'One of the advantages of skin clothing over woollens in Arctic exploration is that you can eat them in an emergency, or feed them to your dogs if the need is not quite so pressing. This puts actual starvation off by a week or so.'
Vilhjalmur Stefansson, the great Manitoba – born Arctic explorer.

After the Loyalists settled in what is now the Maritimes, the grandmother of Sir Samuel Leonard Tilley, Lieutenant-Governor of New Brunswick, is supposed to have said – 'I climbed up the hill, watching the sails disappearing. Such loneliness came over me. Although I had not shed a tear through the war, I sat down on the damp moss with my baby held tight, and cried.'
About 1784.

Muktuk

Muktuk (whale skin) has a rubbery texture and tastes like fried eggs. Delicious eaten raw or fried. Whale meat may best be served as steaks. First remove all fat.

March 2, 1804
Four mutineers and three deserters, of the 6th, 41st, and 49th regiments were executed at Quebec.

March 2, 1956
The white blue-shaded dogwood blossom was named the floral emblem of British Columbia, winning out over the suggested columbine.

March, 1604
Living trees were the supporting pillars of the first place of worship in Canada, on St. Croix Island, Passamaquoddy Bay, N.B. erected by De Monts, along with a fort. When Pierre, Sieur de Monts, a Huguenot and Calvinist, came to the New World, he was to have free exercise of his religion, but was to convert the aborigines to the Catholic faith! The first resident Christian missionary was Nicholas Aubry, a secular priest, who, with 36 other immigrants, died of scurvy during the first wretched winter.

March 1661
In Canada two men were shot and one was whipped for selling brandy to Indians.

March 1813
The 104th regiment, New Brunswick regulars, marched from Federicton to Quebec through the snow-covered wilderness.

MARCH

The oyster bars of the 1860's were always crowded. In Montreal the only thing that folks liked better was to climb aboard the oyster barges in the harbour, where for twenty cents or so, a man was free to eat as many oysters as he could hold. It was the thing to carry one's own special oyster opener, and there was always discussion as to who could open the most in the least time. We are told that 'greats' like Sir John A. Macdonald and Sir Wilfrid Laurier entered into the spirit of these parties with zest and informality.

'A beautiful bird seldom sings'.
'The Clockmaker, or The Sayings and Doings of Samuel Slick, of Slickville', by Justice Thomas Chandler Haliburton, 1836.

Notre Dame de Lourdes, Montreal.

The Chinese came to British Columbia in 1860 before Victoria, Vancouver or New Westminster existed, lured by the California gold mines, which they later abandoned for the richer Fraser Gold strike. Two thousands became expert placer miners and prospectors, all before B.C. joined Confederation in 1871.

In 1881 when cheap plentiful workers were needed for the railway across the Rockies, 17,000 coolies were brought in for the brutally hard labour. They continued to come as millhands, merchants, railway hands and gardeners in native costume and wearing the queue, which they did not cut off until 1900.

However, long, before that – between 458 and 566 A.D. – there were Chinese Buddhist priests in B.C. The Cathay Year Book of that era called the land **Fusang**, which meant The Extreme East, and noted it 'wonderful'.

In the 1200's, a few centuries later, but still well ahead of Christopher Colombus, came the Jews, then very powerful in China. Many Jewish soldiers with Kublai Khan, on his ill-fated attack on Japan, were dispersed by what the Japanese have ever since referred to as The Divine Wind, and their junks drifted to the mouth of the Naas River in B.C.

'There is just one thing in which you excel Canada, I admit, and that is with regard to your northern boundary, for, while you have the greatest nation under the sun as your northern boundary, we must admit we have only the North Pole.' Charles Hopewell, to an ᴀmerican, at Empire Club speech, 1911.

'This is the first time I ever was in a city where you couldn't throw a brick without breaking a church window. When I heard you were going to build still another, I said, 'Where are you going to find room?' I was told, 'We will build it on top of another church with an elevator'.'

Mark Twain, on a lecture tour in Montreal, 1881.

Here in Canada. the Welsh say on St. David's Day:
Eat leeks in July and
    garlic in May
And all the year your
    doctor may play.

Medals, engraved 'For Merit-Presented by a Grateful Country-Upper Canada Preserved' were struck by the Loyal and Patriotic Society of Upper Canada, but never distributed, as the difficulty of deciding who was to receive them was too great. They were defaced and broken up in York early in the 1800's.

When the homesteaders started working the land, they were astonished to find their farm implements stained red, but soon realized that it was caused by the berries that grew so plentifully. There were all kinds – strawberries, raspberries, gooseberries and saskatoons – and they made a mid-morning snack, brought to the workers in the fields.

March used to be the first month of the year until Julius Caesar made it the third when he corrected the old Roman calendar. Named for Martius (Mars) the Roman God of War, it had many other designations, such as 'the boisterous month', 'the windy month' and 'the lengthening month', all for very obvious reasons.

OLD TIMOTHY

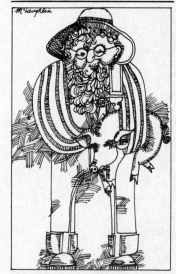

'Find good neighbours an' work hard ef ye wanta giv thanks fer a good long life.'

Quebec and Montreal were the scenes of many lavish and fashionable dinner parties during the French regime. We are told that 'a silver spoon and fork wrapped in a napkin were placed on the left of each plate. Ladies and gentlemen provided their own knives, hung from the neck, in a sheath of morocco, silk or birch bark artistically worked.'

MARCH

The curator of the Graphic Arts Division of the United States National Museum has established that the 'first halftones to appear in any publication' were in 1869 in the first issue of the 'Canadian Illustrated News', Canada's first national news magazine and the first publication anywhere to use letterpress halftone reproductions of photographs. The cover of the first issue carried a photographic portrait of H.R.H. Prince Arthur. George E. Desbarats, the publisher, was ten years ahead of Frederick E. Ives, who patented the first commercially successful letterpress halftone process in the United States.

Sir William Van Horne.   The Public Archives of Canada.

DID YOU KNOW THAT

The High River Pioneers' and Old Timers' Association named its 1960 history 'Leaves From A Medicine Tree' for a beloved tree of very great age near High River, Alberta. An oil painting by B.T. Smith shows Bert Pierson on a spirited bucking horse at the tree, actually two cottonwoods joined some feet above ground, so that their sap ran together. Indian Lovers and warriors left offerings between the two, trunks. They brought the sick and laid the dead nearby for kindly spirits to lead to the Happy Hunting Grounds. There was no evil. Great feasts flourished. For had not the legend promised – 'As each leaf falls it brings to earth a blessing from the Great Spirit, a promise that HERE the grass shall always grow, and man and beasts shall prosper.'

Two of the men of war, the 'Satellite' & 'Plumper' with ourselves, determined to give a grand ball to the ladies of Vancouver Island . . . The ladies were very nicely dressed & some . . . danced very well. They would look much better, if they would only learn to wear their crinolines properly.
Lieut. Charles W. Wilson, Victoria, B.C. March 15, 1859.

Script money issued by Alberta's Social Credit government was in circulation in all sections of the province in 1936. A total of $250,000 in bills with the face value of $1 had been distributed by the Provincial Treasury.

'Almost every day, there is a 'Bee' which takes every other hand away. These 'bees' are getting to be a nuisance, between seed-time and harvest is almost filled with them . . . Some talk of cutting 'Bees' generally, and helping each other with men and cattle for 2 or 3 days at a time'. (1842)

'There was a 'bee' today for making a road up to the church'. (1839)
A Gentlewoman in Upper Canada,' by Anne Langton, 1841.

'If you want anything done, name the day when it must be finished. If I order a thing done in a specified time, and the man to whom I give that order says it is impossible to carry it out, then he must go.'
Sir William C Van Horne, K.C.M.G., President and Chairman of the Board of Directors of the Canadian Pacific Railway (1888-1910).

OLD TIMOTHY

'Never tell folks you can go ahead on 'em, but do it; it spares a great deal of talk and helps to save their breath to cool their broth.'

Mt. Robson, 13,500 feet high, is the highest peak of the Canadian Rockies.

Lake Louise and the Province of Alberta were named for Princess Louise Alberta, wife of the Marquis of Lorne, Governor General of Canada, 1878-83. She was the fourth daughter of Queen Victoria. At the time of her marriage, this story was retold in the Toronto Globe from Punch. One Gael said to another, 'The Queen's young dochter's goin' to be marrit to MacCallum Mohr's son'. To which the other Gael replied, 'Each! Dod, the Queen maun be the proud woman.'

MARCH

March has two exotic birthstones – the clear sea green-to-blue aquamarine and the opaque bloodstone, a strong masculine gem. The aquamarine insures a happy marriage, imparts courage, cures laziness and quickens the intellect. The bloodstone is said to bring wisdom.

DATES OF INTEREST

March 14, 1916
Saskatchewan gives the vote to women.

March 15, 1814
Indians were great orators and enjoyed a 'talk' such as the one with the Governor at Château St. Louis, Quebec. When the chiefs and warriors of the Mohawks, Ottawas, Chippewas, Sacs, Foxes, Shawnees, Kickapoos and Winabagoes departed for the West, they carried away many, many presents.

March 15, 1843
The first priest, Father Bolduc, landed on Vancouver Island. Practically simultaneously James Douglas, with 15 men, began building Fort Camosun (Victoria) the first settlement work on the Island.

To make Celaphalic Snuff.

1. Grind equal parts asarabacca leaves, marjoram, and light snuff. Grind. Sift the resulting powder.
2. Take 1 pound powdered asarum, 1½ pounds powdered dry Scotch snuff, 2 pounds simple powder, 4 ounces of hellebore. Mix. Sift.

14 families, Indian and Half Breeds settled near the Prince Albert Mission, making 106 inhabitants. 22 Indian and Half Breed Children attend the school which is too small. A person with a knowledge of English and Cree is very much wanted to teach. *The Winnipeg 'Manitoban', March 4, 1871.*

Judge Emily Murphy   *The Public Archives of Canada.*

OUR GRASS ROOTS

The Provincial of the Jesuits in Quebec in 'Jesuit Relations', 1636, mentions that the farm labourers receive flour, lard, oil, vinegar, codfish, peas and 'a chopine of cider a day, or a quart of beer.'

Two years earlier, Father Le Jeune, the first superior of the order in Canada, said 'We shall have to make some beer; and build a brewery'. In 1646 at a religious celebration, the crafts were represented in this order in the procession – 'carpenters, masons, sailors, toolmakers, brewers and bakers'.

When Intendant Jean Talon decided to build a brewery in 1668, Father Francis Le Mercier, S.J., wrote from Quebec – 'This will force a decrease in the use of intoxicating drinks. Moreover it will keep in the country the money now sent to purchase much liquor in France. It will use the super-abundance of grain.'

Brewing, Canada's oldest manufacturing industry, has since the end of World War II paid $2,800,000,000 in taxes.

From an Almanac of 1847.
Query 'Is it not better to keep stock at the barn late in the spring, rather than permit them to feed down meadow land?'
Answer: 'Certainly! Farmers err much in allowing cattle to run over their meadow land or pasture before the ground is settled or the grass started. Animals should be fed at the barn till there is a pretty fair bite of grass.'

ARE WOMEN PERSONS?

She was a person herself, and she settled for all time the fact that all women are persons. For Judge Emily Murphy was of the 'Famous Five' (the others being Mrs. Nellie L. McClung, also of Edmonton, Mrs. Irene Parlby, Mrs. Louise McKinney and Mrs. O. C. Edwards, all of Alberta) whose efforts resulted in a 1929 decision by the Privy Council in London, England, that women could sit in the Senate.

The Privy Council decision overturned a Supreme Court of Canada ruling that women are not 'persons' in the sense of being able to sit in the Senate.

Although Judge Murphy was recommended widely as the best choice for the first Canadian woman senator, she was not appointed. A veteran Senator remarked, 'O, we couldn't have Mrs. Murphy in the Senate! She would have stirred up too much trouble.'

As 'Janey Canuck' this remarkable crusader wrote extensively of her experiences, for she was the first woman in the British Empire to be appointed a Police Magistrate.

MARCH

The 'Canadian Illustrated News' (1880) was all for a combination of surah satin and religeuse veiling for summer evening dresses with draping, pleating and flouncing of the semi-diaphanous material. Afternoon frocks were to have parasols and fans to match. For Easter, the hats and bonnets were larger and fancier, with everybody mad for a creation called the 'English Gypsy', a little number with a 'netted cord, covering the turned up back brim'.

The Ottawa 'Daily Citizen' (1879) told of 3-button kid gloves at 50 cents the pair, and reminded the ladies that colours for spring were pale blue, cream, ecru, grenat, and mastic.

Big Alex McDonald, whose Yukon fortune ran into eight figures, was married in London, England to a Miss Margaret Chisholm. The happy bride of the King of the Klondike probably does not know that her name may have attracted her rich husband. For it was a Miss Margaret Chisholm, of Dawson, who was the first pretty girl that Big Alex saw when he returned from the mines. The King left Dawson with a letter for Police Supt. Chisholm in London. He did not look further when he heard there was a 20-year-old Margaret.

When Miss Margaret Chisholm, of Dawson, heard of the marriage of her English namesake, she said, 'It's all in the family.'

OLD TIMOTHY

'When the wimmin folk, inside, don't help the men folk, outside, the house ends up leanin' towards the road.'

●●●●●●●●●●●●●●●●●●●●●●●●●●●

While still a child, François de Malepart Beaucourt was taught to paint by his painter-engineer father. At 32, he left Laprairie, Quebec, where he was born in 1740, for Paris and Bordeaux for further study. His portrait of 'A Negro Slave' is in the National Gallery at Ottawa.

The first Jewish settlers.
In 1751, four Hart brothers settled near the naval base at Halifax, N.S. On March 20, 1793, Samuel Hart was the first Jew to be elected M.L.A. of Nova Scotia, representing Liverpool, a small town near Halifax, for 6 years.

These Harts were not related to Aaron Hart, formerly a lieutenant in the British Army, who settled near Three Rivers, Quebec, in 1760. The second post office established in Canada was in his home.

Martyrdom of Jesuit Missionaries. *The Public Archives of Canada.*

OUR GRASS ROOTS

If we are to judge by Montreals fire station's of 1840, the fire fighters were not only stalwart and brave, but very romantic as well. Ten stations, placed strategically about the city, which was in constant fear of fire, had personalities and names all their own. The Hero was on St. Joseph Street; The Protector on Notre Dame Street; The Neptune on St. Mary Street, The Phoenix on St. Lawrence Blvd., and La France close to the Harbour.

Squares in Montreal have been named for Gilles Hocquart, an intendant of New France, who founded the City's first fire brigade two and a half centuries ago; and for Director Raoul Gauthier who was killed fighting a harbour fire aboard the ship **Cymbeline** in 1932.

Two hundred Persian families are expected in the Battleford, Sask., district in the spring. The Presbyterians are sending a Nestorian missionary to the people.

At the martyrdom of Father Jean de Bréboeuf in the country of the Hurons, March 1649, the Iroquois tormented him, saying –

'Thou seest plainly that we treat thee as a friend, since we shall be the cause of thy Eternal happiness; thank us, then, for these good offices which we render thee, for the more thou shalt suffer, the more will thy God reward thee.'

'The water wagon is certainly a more dangerous vehicle than the automobile. At least more people fall off it.'
'Calgary Eye Opener'.

The early pioneers in Alberta were proud of the name 'Old-Timer'. You might say politely to a man on the street, 'Good morning, sir,' and he'd keep on walking; but if you said, 'Good morning, Old-Timer,' he'd know you were the right kind and stop for a chat.

DATES OF INTEREST

March 17, 1810
A magistrate, 2 constables and some soldiers, suppressed **Le Canadien**, in Quebec, in an arbitrary proceeding.

March 17, 1866.
Volunteers were under arms all day, fearing a Fenian invasion of Upper Canada.

March 18, 1885.
In an uprising at Duck Lake, the Métis started the Northwest Rebellion fighting. They imprisoned the Indian agent, seized public stores, and killed 14 policemen.

'It is far more to Canada's advantage than ours to be on good terms with us. Lord Salisbury in a private conversation the other day compared her to a coquettish girl with two suitors, playing one off against the other. I would think a closer analogy would be to call her a married flirt, ready to betray John Bull on any occasion, but holding him responsible for all her follies.'

John Hay, U.S. ambassador to London, letter to John W. Foster, 1897.

Crows
One for sorrow,
Two for mirth,
The third a wedding
And fourth a birth.
Old New Brunswick superstition.

A candle burnt to the socket
Brings luck to the house
Food to the larder
And gold to the pocket.
Old Upper Canada rhyme.

The Joker of the Parish.

DID YOU KNOW THAT

'Ague and lake fever had attacked our new settlement ... Those who have drawn such agreeable pictures of a residence in the backwoods, never dwell upon the periods of sickness, when far from medical advice, and often, as in my case, deprived of the assistance of friends by adverse circumstances, you are left to languish, unattended, upon the couch of pain.

'My husband and I had worked hard in the field; it was the first time I had ever tried my hand at field-labour, but our money was exhausted ... I had a hard struggle with my pride before I would consent to render the least assistance on the farm, but reflection convinced me that I was wrong' ... Susanna Moodie, 1885.

'In Canada, we have enough to do keeping up with two spoken languages without trying to invent slang, so we just go right ahead and use English for literature, Scotch for sermons, and American for conversations.' *Stephen Leacock.*

Old Glory, a 450 year old sugar maple, that was a century old when Champlain came to Canada in 1603, still spreads its huge branches at North Pelham in the Niagara Peninsula. In 1946, the Comfort family sold their farm, acquired in 1816, but not the plot on which the tree stands, 90 feet tall.

Everybody knows that when the Irish get together they raise their voices in song. First of course toasts are drunk traditionally with a pint of Guiness draught stout, or a lighter lager called Harp. The songs are just as likely to be these same ones that were popular years back –
'Kitty of Colerain'
'Grammachree Molly'
'Cushla machree'
'The Bridge of Athlone'
'The Walls of Limerick'
'Let Erin Remember the Days of Old'
'Canadian Boat Song'
'Granuwale'
'The Oak Stick'
'The Coulin'
'Sprig of Shillelagh'

'God has saved my life many times, therefore I must give Him the praise.'
Thomas Molson, 1852.

'A short feast and a long famine' referred in Newfoundland to the vicissitudes of fishing. In the fall of the year, the catch was sold to Spain, Portugal and the West Indies, and the vessels returned with abundant fruits and wine, and food was bought for the long winter. Famine time was March and April, and sometimes May, if the drift ice bottled the harbours.

The Northwest Territories, Canada's vast northland of 1,304,903 square miles, will become our eleventh province in 1978. This is something that the nine members of the NWT Council have been discussing in Ottawa. Although the population is about 26,000 the land involved is 34% of Canada's total.

The man-about-town in Montreal had a choice of many good restaurants and hotels in the late 1700's and the 1800's. Most of them were not too far from the harbour, and did well by the travelling public. People gathered for business and for social assemblies. Among the most popular were The Mansion House, the Hummums, (named after the fashionable hotel in Covent Garden, London), Rasco's, on St. Paul Street, St. Lawrence Hall, on St. James Street and the Exchange Hotel and Coffee Shop.

It has been said that the proud bold Indians shaved their heads bald, leaving just a single scalp-lock as a challenge to their enemies, be they white men or Indians. This single lock threatened, 'Cut my scalp-lock off, **if you dare!'**

DATES OF INTEREST

March 25, 1780
The British Government decreed that this be celebrated as Lady Day, the Feast of the Annunciation, in Canada. In medieval times Lady Day was the beginning of the legal year, a practice that terminated in 1752. However March 25 remained a 'quarter day'.

March 25, 1880
Hon. George Brown, editor, was shot in the Toronto **Globe** office by George Bennett, a discharged employee.

March 26, 1897
Bob Edwards, of 'Calgary Eye Opener' fame, brought out the first issue of his Wetaskiwin Free Lance, the first paper published between Calgary and Edmonton.

78th Regiment of Foot. 1759. *The Public Archives of Canada.*

... 'The Hare Indians who inhabit this country are distinguished from all other tribes by one honourable peculiarity, the women do no labour whatever, the duties of the household are all performed by men: this cannot be in deference to their charms, for they are the ugliest of mortals, nor for their amiability, for they make no scruple in devouring their husbands and children when pressed by famine.'

'In Search of the Magnetic Pole' by John Henry Lefroy, a soldier-surveyor's letters from the North West, 1843-44. Courtesy of Dr. Gustav Lanctot.

The 'state of subscription in favour of the Poor' issued by Hôtel Dieu, March 30, 1784, in Quebec City, showed that £345, 10s, 9d, had been collected. His Excellency General Haldimand headed the list with £50. Hôtel Dieu, the first hospital in America, north of Mexico, was founded in 1639.

The notice went on to say that the 'sick person is treated kindly...his feet are washed, he has clean sheets which are changed once a month, and oftener if necessary, and his shifts once a week.' Charitable people were asked for wood, old linens, meat, bread, wine, vinegar, rice, raisins and sugar.

DID YOU KNOW THAT

The Aroostook War was largely concerned with the boundaries of New Brunswick, which had not been clearly defined by the treaty of 1783. March 25, 1839 marked a compromise, and later an agreement was reached between Lord Ashburton and the eminent American jurist, Daniel Webster. Of the many war songs, the Americans shouted this one lustily –
We'll lick the red-coats anyhow,
And drive them from our border;
The loggers are awake – and all
Await the Gin'ral's order;
Britannia shall not rule the Maine,
Nor shall she rule the water;
They've sung that song full long enough,
Much longer than they ougher.

It was Simon Fraser who raised the 78th regiment which first saw service in 1758 at Louisbourg. The French Canadians called the Fraser Highlanders 'Les Sauvages d'Ecosse', or 'Les Petites Jupes'. It was said that they fought 'with streaming plaids, bonnets and large swords – like so many infuriated demons.'

Our great-grandmothers learned to make an efficacious dressing for injuries with crushed plantain leaves. They found that smartweed, steeped in vinegar, was excellent for the treatment of bruises.

MARCH

Everything is bigger in the N.W.T. Canada's highest peak, Mount Logan in the St. Elias chain, has an elevation of 19,850 feet. Her longest river, the Mackenzie, runs for 2,635 miles into the Arctic through the N.W.T. The biggest island, Baffin Land, has an area of 178,000 square miles, and the highest big lake, Kusawa, is 2,565 above sea level.

In 1800 it was a common sight at vacation time to note students trudging home to Montreal from the Quebec Seminary, a journey of a week on foot. The young men hoped for a welcome at farm houses, otherwise they stopped at any of the twenty-four post houses on the route.

'Wealth from the Sea, E Mari Merces' is the Halifax motto. From 1604 when French captains, Pontgravé and Morell, built the first ship in Canada or New England, at Louisbourg, the story of Halifax is the story of ships. Probably the best loved was the fishing schooner and racer, the Bluenose, launched at Lunenburg, on March 26, 1921. The graceful design of this famous Queen of the North Atlantic, this champion of its fishing fleets, is seen on a ten cent coin and on a special postage stamp issued in 1929. Dedicated to her memory, Bluenose II, was launched in the same shipyard in 1963. Although built from the same original plans she will never race.

Sir John William Dawson, Men of Canada, 1901-1902.
The Public Archives of Canada.

Sir William Dawson, Principal of McGill University, said of it in 1855 – 'It consisted of two blocks of unfinished and partly ruinous buildings, standing amid a wilderness of excavator's and mason's rubbish, overgrown with weeds and bushes. The grounds were unfenced and pastured at will by herds of cattle. The only access from the town was by a circuitous and ungraded cart track, almost unpassable at night.'

'There is a way of doin' everything, if you only know how to go about it'.

Justice Thomas Chandler Haliburton, 'Sam Slick's Wise Saws', 1853.

OLD TIMOTHY

'Western Injuns (like Injuns everywhere) wuz confirmed gamblers – especially on hawss races. A redskin would bet his squaw, his tepee, his ponies and his buckskins, and losing all, might even bet his scalp.'

An ancient cure for deafness:

Have the fat from the Kidneys of wild Rabbit; gridel it out and put in two drops in each ear, each night; rub cotton batting to a point, dip it in the Immediate Relief, and put it in the ear. Let it remain till better.

'Mrs. Palmer's Home Remedy Book', about 1832.

The remarkable Bishop John Strachan was spoken of by Thomas Carlyle, as 'the turbulent priest of Toronto.'

OUR GRASS ROOTS

Homesickness and pride of origin influenced settlers to give old-country names. It was the English who named London, Ontario, seeing it as the future metropolis for all of Canada. With memories of the craggy cliffs on the North Sea, they labelled Scarborough, Ontario, in 1792. Edmonton, Alberta, bears the name of the town near London, of John Gilpin fame.

   'Thus all through merry Islington
   These gambols did he play,
   Until he came upon the Wash
   Of Edmonton so gay.'

Edmonton got its real start in the 1897-98 Klondike Gold Rush, growing from a few hundred to several thousands. Claims that it was the best, quickest and easiest road to the gold were misleading, for only one in 500 arrived that way. Edmonton really made it during the last war. It was the 'last chance town', the jumping-off place for the Alaska Highway construction and other northern projects.

SPRING

APRIL

April

Pale season, watcher in unvexed suspense.
Still priestess of the patient middle day,
Betwixt wild March's humoured petulance
And the warm wooing of green kirtled May,
Maid month of sunny peace and sober grey,
Weaver of flowers in sunward glades that ring
With murmur of libation to the spring.

Archibald Lapman, born in 1861 in Morpeth, Ont., and died aged 38.

Legend has it that our Indians discovered maple syrup centuries ago when a squaw, too lazy to walk to the stream for water, used tree sap for boiling venison. Her warrior husband found the taste extremely pleasant and they experimented by dropping hot stones into the sap to make a strong, thick, dark, smoky (and probably very impure) syrup and sugar.

It was not until 1673 that a French priest wrote his superior in France about maple sap. Although there is no doubt that they copied the natives and tapped the trees, there is no authentic record of maple products until 1706.

OLD TIMOTHY

'Folks usta say
it wuz soon enuff to shake
hands with the Divil when
you met face to face.'

Boiling the Sap.

A slide loaned to the Public Archives of Canada.

On April First one of the favourite Scottish tricks was to send someone to a friend's house with a note reading

'This day of April Fool we smile,
Send this Fool another mile'.

Often the word 'gowk' was substituted for fool, gowk meaning a cuckoo.

The French Canadian calls it **poisson d'Avril,** which probably signifies that fish is not always the favourite food.

In the eastern provinces the superstitious hold that

'A thunderstorm on All Fools' Day
Is good for crops of corn and hay.'

In the west however, they believe a foggy April First foretells floods.

One cannot help regarding with some suspicion the way in which the City Council has dealt, and is dealing with the Water Works question. Why is discussion shunned? Why is it staved off from week to week? Why is not some conclusion come to, instead of allowing the subject to sleep?

'Daily Mail', Toronto, April 6, 1872.

OUR GRASS ROOTS

The search for buried treasure seems to have entered the realm of big business. In the spring of 1966, three Nova Scotia divers recovered a hoard of gold and silver coins, estimated to be worth $700,000, from the submerged wreck of Le Chameau, a French pay ship which sank fifteen miles off Louisbourg in 1725.

What happens when an expedition of this kind comes off successfully? Before one can read the words on a single **louis d'or,** the scene is overrun with sheriffs, injunctions, federal, provincial and municipal officials, lawyers, coin collectors, newspaper and magazine reporters, radio and T.V. personnel. This particular salvage of Le Chameau even brought forth another contestant. A Portuguese skipper claims the ship and the booty, saying that he recovered from it, in 1961, three large iron and two small brass cannons.

The cost of living has increased during the past three years, say our Government friends. Quite true. It always does when times are good. *Fredericton 'Capital', April, 1882.*

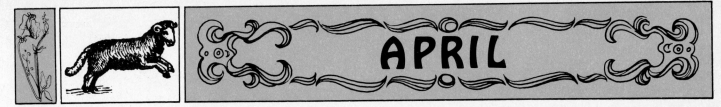

APRIL

When our early settlers were clearing the land, neighbours came from miles around to help one another, in the form of a 'bee' which combined voluntary labour and a social event. We read of house-raising bees, barn-raising bees, quilting-bees, apple-paring bees and many others. The hosts provided the best they could in the way of food.

Some bees were more social, but the logging-bee was rather rough. J. M. D. Moodie, husband of Susanna Moodie, who wrote 'Roughing it in the Bush', tells us in verse about his logging-bee to which thirty-two strong men were invited. Cooking went on for three days before. The menu included pea soup, venison, eels, legs of pork, potatoes, raspberry pies, tea and whiskey.

'He who drinks Red River water once, must drink it again.' This saying of the North West in 1880 still holds true, despite the fact that the 'raging, flood-swollen Red' threatens its valleys in Manitoba each April. Flood control authorities watch its dikes, meteorologists report the cresting of the rise, emergency crews stand by ready to help if evacuation is necessary — yet they all love the river.

'Will you share my lot, dearest?' whispered the Calgary lover. 'I will', cooed the Reginan, 'if it's a Regina lot; because you know, dear, they've gone up!'
'The Leader', Regina, April, 1905.

DATES OF INTEREST

April 2, 1885
Indians massacre whites at Frog Lake, Alta. All but two lie buried at Onion Lake cemetery. Fathers Fafard and Marchand were buried in the Oblate Plot at St. Albert Mission, established in 1861 by Father Lacombe who did much to keep peace between whites and Indians.

April, 1757-8
Famine in Quebec with daily bread rations of two ounces. Horse meat eaten until relief from France in May. Three hundred Acadians died of starvation.

April 4, 1784
The first marriage in New Brunswick took place at Parr Town, now Saint John, when Lieutenant Andrew Stockton, formerly of New Jersey, took a Loyalist bride.

April, 1630
La Tour and his son received 4,500 square miles in Nova Scotia from Sir William Alexander.

April 5, 1669
King Louis XIV, of France, by Royal Decree, conferred distinction and monetary gifts upon parents of large families in Canada. The happy father of 10 legitimate children received a pension of 300 livres; of 12 was given 400 livres. The largest families were given positions of honour.

There was a man in our town,
In our town, in our town,
There was a man in our town,
He made a logging-bee.
And he bought lots of whiskey,
To make the loggers frisky,
To make the loggers frisky,
At his logging-bee.

The Devil sat on a log heap,
A log heap, a log heap,
A red hot burning log heap,
A-grinning at the bee;
And there was lots of swearing,
Of boasting and of daring,
Of fighting and of tearing
At that logging bee.

The April birth flowers are the daisy, meaning simplicity and innocence, and the sweet pea, signifying modesty.

'Tremprette' is a dessert of days gone by that is still very popular in the Province of Quebec. Crusty, flavourful French bread is dunked in real maple syrup and eaten with heavy country cream.

In Nova Scotia 'a blueberry grunt' is a rich pie and 'Digby chicks' are smoked herrings.

Forty gallons of sap makes one gallon of the precious maple syrup or ten pounds of the delicious sugar.

DID YOU KNOW THAT

Funeral of D'Arcy McGee, Montreal, 1868. The Public Archives of Canada.

Thoughts of early violent death haunted Thomas D'Arcy McGee, a Father of Confederation and one of our most brilliant orators and writers who died at forty-two from an assassin's bullet. His poem 'Forewarned' reads:

'In the time of my boyhood I had a strange feeling,
That I was to die in the noon of my day,
Not quietly into the silent grave stealing,
But torn, like a blasted oak, suddenly away.'

Four years before his death, he wrote of 'Fenianism' – 'Even the threat of assassination, covertly conveyed and so eminently in keeping with the entire humbug, has no terrors for me. I trust I shall outlive these threats.' On April 7, 1868, he was killed by a Fenian, Patrick James Whelan. Sixty thousand people crowded the streets of Montreal to show D'Arcy McGee honour and respect, twenty thousand of the mourners marching behind the hearse.

APRIL

Once Thomas D'Arcy McGee decided to become a Canadian, he gave up his criticism of England. Before a Montreal audience, he said – 'I hold we have no right to intrude our Irish patriotism on this soil; for our first duty is to the land where we live . . . and where . . . we must find the true sphere of our duties. While always ready therefore to say the right word, and do the right act for the land of my forefathers, I am bound above all to the land where I reside; and . . . to put down . . . the insensate spread of a strife which can only tend to prolong our period of provincialism and make the country an undesirable home for those who would otherwise cast in their lot among us.'

Dainty and sweet
As the gay spring flowers,
The babe that is born
In April showers.

Thomas D'Arcy Mc.Gee. The Public Archives of Canada.

DATES OF INTEREST

April 8, 1751
William Pigott, of Halifax, N.S., opened the first Inn in Canada for English speaking travellers.

April 8, 1841
Anne Langton, 'a gentlewoman of Upper Canada', wrote – 'The election has taken place, but the candidate for whom all our young men voted, did not succeed in obtaining his election. John had to walk seventy or eighty miles to give his vote, sleeping where he could, and returned half-famished and very much fatigued.'

April 8, 1941
Saskatchewan adopted the orange-red wildwood or prairie lily, also known as the tiger lily, as its floral emblem. A second emblem, the prairie chicken or sharp-tailed grouse, was adopted in 1945.

April 9, 1682
The quarrels between haughty Jacques Duchesneau, Intendant of New France, and proud and overbearing Frontenac, the Governor, became intolerable to the King, who recalled them. Many merchants and priests (excepting the Recollet Fathers) rejoiced, but the men in the street felt they needed Frontenac's protection in times of danger.

April 13, 1825
Arriving at the Port of Lunenburgh, Nova Scotia, were schooners 'Morning Star' (Capt. Moser) from Dominica and 'Lady' (Capt. Ernst) from Newfoundland.

DID YOU KNOW THAT

It might surprise a Canadian to find the Wigwam Bar, Nevins St., Brooklyn, crowded with Mohawk Indians. These are the élite of high-steel construction, the skilful, fearless riveters. Over 400 from the Caughnawagha Reservation, ten miles from Montreal, have practically taken over a whole city block in Brooklyn. They have worked on the George Washington Bridge, New York, the Golden Gate Bridge, San Francisco, the Empire State Building, New York, and similar structures around the world. These Indians came to high steel by accident, when Dominion Bridge Company officials noticed them using the narrow girders on the bridge under construction near the reservation as a short cut. That was in 1886, and since then they are first choice for the most dangerous jobs. They have no acrophobia (fear of high places) and have a real zest for their daring work. Like their forefathers, who crossed Canada by canoe, they always return to Caughnawagha.

Stormy day, one soldier Dyed last night Belonging to Capt. Hobbs Company the first yt has Dyed since they were mustered at Boston.
Diary of Surgeon Thomas, of Lt.-Col. John Winslow's forces in Acadia, April, 1755.

Nova Scotia had the first circulating library in Canada, in 1812.

Establishing and maintaining 'Strathcona's Horse' at his own expense for service in the South African War was just the kind of thing that Sir Donald Alexander Smith (Lord Strathcona) would do. In his vigorous life, this man who wanted to be a lawyer but couldn't afford the years of study, was a successful fur-trader, politician and financier. Immensely wealthy, he gave millions to the Royal Victoria Hospital, McGill University, The Royal Victoria College for Women (who were all called Donaldas, after him) and many other institutions.

The diamond, April's birthstone, is a victory talisman, said to endow the wearer with superior strength, fortitude and courage. It's 'fire that never dies out' diverts the evil eye.

Those who in April
Start their years,
Diamonds should wear,
Lest salty tears
In sorrow flow.
This stone
A gem
Of innocence is known.

'Don't put your tongue in high until you get your brain started.'
Jack Miner, O.B.E.

APRIL

Sir Wilfred Grenfell, the medical missionary, was to speak on his work in Labrador at a banquet in Toronto. Arriving late, he explained that he had navigated from his hotel by the stars, but it hadn't worked out quite right.

'We are in the rapids and must go on.'

Thomas D'Arcy McGee
Confederation debates, 1865.

April rains for men (giving corn), May rains for beasts (giving grass).

An old saying from New Brunswick farm-lands.

'Books only weaken your understandin' as water does brandy.'

Justice Thomas Chandler Haliburton, 'The Clockmaker, or The Sayings and Doings of Samuel Slick of Slickville', 1838.

'When a man has done me an evil turn once, I don't like to give him the opportunity to do so twice.'

Sir John A. Macdonald.

Notice is hereby given that Abijah Durkee played cards with Thomas L. Gilbert in said Gilbert's Tavern, till said Durkee had won 4 dollars, which the said Gilbert refused to pay. This is therefore to caution against sporting with said gambler. Abijah Durkee, Lime, U.C., March 19, 1801.

'Every government selected for the civil service their own friends, and no one could object to it'.
Sir John A. Macdonald, House of Commons Debates, April, 1878.

The Legislature of Prince Edward Island, established in 1773, is held to be one of the oldest on the whole American continent.

Four different coloured pencils were used to mark the ballots, when four candidates contested a by-election at Whitehood, near Regina, about 1893. Voters were instructed to use the pencil of the colour assigned to his favourite. All went well until a frienzied communication to Regina indicated that Fairmede poll had only three pencils. The missing pencil was expressed on a C.P.R. train to Whitewood. There in a raging blizzard, liveryman Fred Chamberlain waited with a fresh, fast horse and took possession of the precious cargo — one coloured pencil. Through storm and dark, he whipped his steed for the last hazardous twenty-five miles, and got to the poll before it opened.

The Strange Holey Dollar of P.E.I.

Back in the 1700's, the Spanish Government minted a large silver coin, the widely-circulated 'Spanish Dollar'. Because its value was highest in Halifax, P.E.I. merchants sent them there, leaving a coin shortage on The Island.

To cope with this situation, Charles Douglas Smith, the Lieutenant-Governor from 1812-24, gathered in all he could, and had the centres punched out. The centre rounds passed as shillings, the outer rims as five dollars. Since they were not accepted elsewhere, the mutilated coins remained on The Island.

But that is not the whole story. A shrewd Scotsman, named Birnie, found that the punched out bits contained nearly two dollars worth of silver, and sent a large collection to his account in London. Alas, the ship was lost. Are the silver pieces still at the bottom of the Atlantic?

OLD TIMOTHY

'Folks usta say, spring ain't come until ye kin put yer foot on a dozen daisies at onct.'

A visitor to Charlottetown, in the early days, said, 'I found Charlottetown to be wicked enough for a far larger place.'

OUR GRASS ROOTS

It all started in 1606 at Port Royal, when they read and discussed the books that Marc Lescarbot was proud to lend, and at Quebec, when children gathered in 1620 to have Marie Rollet Hébert read to them. Today, centuries later, Library Week is marked in April throughout the provinces.

At the beginning, there was a Jesuit Library in Quebec in 1635, library donations by John Graves Simcoe to the Upper Canada Legislature in 1791, a Law Library in Halifax in 1797, and the Library Association and Mechanics Institute Act in 1851.

In 1876 the Library of Parliament was opened in its pure Gothic beauty. Styled like the Reading Room in the British Museum, there are 500,000 books available, some dating back to before 1800.

Talked about since Confederation, the National Library came into being on Jan. 1, 1953. The new building on Wellington Street is the main part of our system that extends across the land, with travelling libraries that deliver their precious cargoes by planes, boats, toboggans, and dog-sleds to isolated areas.

Hop Beer
One handful hops, boil an hour, strain. Add one pint molasses and enough water to make two gallons. When milk-warm, add one cup or cake of yeast. Let stand over night, skim and pour it off from the yeast carefully. Add one tablespoon wintergreen. Bottle for use.

Mrs. Dickinson, Home Cook Book, 50th edition, Toronto, 1877.

A remedy for sciatica and rheumatism.

Rub the painful parts with stinging nettles until red, then bathe with white wine. Repeat several times. 'Almanach de Quebec', 1780.

The movement of the St. Louis Bar in favour of wearing black silk gowns in court meets with acceptance. The 'Law Journal says 'We do not advocate a return to the costume of the English judges and barristers of the middle ages – to wigs, coils, caps, bands and collars; or even to green, red, blue or purple bags... But use of the robe and the gown would add lustre, distinction and gravity to the bench and bar, and would be an incentive to all wearers of these professional insignia to render themselves worthy of distinction'.

DID YOU KNOW THAT

Rudyard Kipling called Medicine Hat the town 'with all hell for a basement', referring to the huge fields of natural gas upon which it stands. When the city fathers were thinking of changing the name, he wrote, 'To my mind the name of Medicine Hat... echoes the old Cree and Blackfoot tradition of red mystery and romance that once filled the prairies... that hints at the magic that underlies your city in the shape of natural gas. Believe me, this very name is an asset. It has no duplicate... It makes men ask questions, and as I knew more than twenty years ago, draws the feet of young men... Above all, it is the lawful, original, sweat- and dust-won name of the city, and to change it would be to risk the luck of the city; to disgust and dishearten old-timers, not in the city alone, but the world over, and to advertise abroad the city's lack of faith in itself.'

How did Medicine Hat come by its name? A great God told a Cree Indian Chief to sacrifice his beloved wife. The God then had him pick up the Medicine Man's Bag or Hat (the Indian word is the same for both) which held good fortune tokens. He became a great warrier and led his tribe to success. From then on, the district was called Medicine Hat.

Angus MacAskill and Tom Thumb. The Cape Breton Giant Gillis, Halifax. 1919. The Public Archives of Canada

Tom Thumb jigged on his palm.

The giant of Cape Breton, Angus MacAskill was 7 foot 9 inches tall and weighed 700 pounds, with shoulders 3 feet 8 inches across. His hands were a foot long and 6 inches wide. His boots had 18 inch soles.

Before the middle 1800's, he performed amazing feats of logging and ploughing. On a circus tour Tom Thumb, the midget, danced on his palm. Queen Victoria invited him to Windsor Castle, where he pressed his heels into the royal carpet, shredding it. The Queen was not amused.

At home in St. Ann's, his favourite stool, a 180 gallon molasses puncheon faced the 9 foot tall door of his store so that he could see his two grist mills.

Lifting a 2,200 lb. anchor from a wharf in New York caused his early death at 38. One of the flukes caught in his shoulder and caused complications. His tomb inscription reads 'Mark the perfect man and beyond the upright, the end of that man is peace.'

The gifted eccentric writer, James D. Gillis, also from Cape Breton, immortalized him in 'The Cape Breton Giant', a unique work that is now a collector's item.

DATES OF INTEREST

April 20, 1534
In the cathedral at St. Malo, France, Jacques Cartier and 60 men took an oath of loyalty to King Francis I and within 3 weeks found themselves in their little ship at the mouth of the St. Lawrence River at the Strait of Belle Isle. There Cartier took possession of the land for France erecting a 30 foot cross and a bright shield ornamented with the fleur-de-lis and the inscription 'Vive le Roy de France'. By Sept. 5, he was back in the harbour of St. Malo, well content with his 4½ months **work.**

Westmount, a beautiful residential area within the limits of Montreal, was incorporated as a city on April 25, 1908. Growing pains took it through these various stages and names:

1874 Village of Notre Dame de Grace

1879 Village of Cote St. Antoine

1890 Town of Cote St. Antoine

1895 Town of Westmount.

Receipt for mending china. Boil piece of flint glass in river water for 3 or 4 minutes. Pound and grind fine as possible on a painter's slab. Mix with whites of eggs to a paste. China so mended with this will never break again in the same place. This method was used by the Chinese.

Winnipeg has entered into a new contract for illuminating with the electric light. *Ottawa 'Daily Citizen', April 1882.*

Rain and sun
Both together
April weather.

Frosty nights and warm sun,
Make the maple sap run.
Ontario Farmers' saying.

April 17, 1886
During a terrible Montreal flood, 'ferry service' at five cents each carried marooned people from the foot of Beaver Hall Hill to St. James Street. The waters reached 5 feet, 10 inches above the revetment wall before abating.

Montreal Flood, April 1886. The Public Archives of Canada.

Our First French Canadian Millionaire.

A Montreal merchant announced in 1803 that he had a position for a sober, industrious, honest man. Walking over fifteen miles from Ste. Eustache, twelve year old Joseph Masson came for the job. Some two decades later, when the business was in difficulties, the Scottish and English creditors put Masson in charge. All debts were paid. Masson even voyaged to Europe to settle some accounts.

Joseph Masson, the Seigneur of Terrebonne, died a millionaire in 1847. He would have been proud of his son, The Hon. Rodrigue Masson, who became Lieutenant-Governor of Quebec in 1884.

OLD TIMOTHY

Out west, nobody ast a new hand nothin' 'bout himself. When the foreman hired him, he sed, 'Now what do ye want us to call ye?'

⚜ ⚜ ⚜ ⚜ ⚜ ⚜ ⚜ ⚜ ⚜

A 'dust devil' is a Canadian expression for a small whirlwind.

⚜ ⚜ ⚜ ⚜ ⚜ ⚜ ⚜ ⚜ ⚜

Stock of Medicines for a Family.

1 oz. of the Emetic Herb (Lobelia)

2 ozs. of Cayenne

½ lb. of Bayberry Root Bark in powder

1 lb. of Poplar Bark

1 lb. of Ginger

1 pt. of Rheumatic Drops (high wines, brandy, gum myrrh and cayenne).

OUR GRASS ROOTS

When Sieur Pierre du Calvet, 18th century fortune seeker and traitor, constructed a secret cellar in his stone house on St. Paul Street, Montreal, opposite the historic Notre-Dame-de-Bon-Secours Church, he had in mind a safe place where he and his fellows could plot undiscovered. Outwardly an ardent Frenchman, Calvet sold information and supplies to the American invaders, was arrested and spent three years in prison. In 1784, he tried to vindicate himself in a pamphlet, 'L'Appel à la Justice de l'Etat', which was distributed in London in English and French.

When he died by shipwreck in 1786 en route to Europe, he left a large estate in Montreal. The architecturally interesting two hundred year old house was bought and restored by Jas. A. Ogilvy's department store to mark its one hundredth birthday anniversary in 1966.

In the cellar where traitors gathered in 1758, friends meet for meals in the French tradition.

DATES OF INTEREST

April 19, 1775
Beginning of American Revolution, Canada remains loyal to Great Britain.

April 20, 1760
7,000 French troops try to recapture Quebec.

April 20, 1836
A company was incorporated to erect a suspension bridge over the Niagara River.

April 23, 1827
John Galt arrived at York, and within 5 days chose Guelph, then unbroken wilderness, as local headquarters of the Canada Company.

APRIL

Pioneer French Canadians, not knowing that the Indians called their game 'baggataway', dubbed it lacrosse because the stick resembled a bishop's crozier or cross.

'Canada is a country with coal-fields at both ends and the railways in between.'

Anonymous.

Clocks will need adjustment to Daylight Saving Time schedules. A good rule is –

Spring forward
Fall back.

Where the change occurs, it is usually the last Sunday in April. Better check.

Only one province remained on Standard Time all year round. Alberta, where Daylight Saving Time has been forbidden since 1948 may now legally demand a provincial plebiscite on the adoption of Daylight Time.

The Gaspé region in Quebec, which is in the Atlantic Time zone, also stayed on Standard Time all the year round.

Cree Indians call April Nis-kepesim, 'goose moon'. Others named it the "green grass moon".

April, the lovely month of burgeoning, is named from the Latin 'aperire', to open; or for 'Aphrilis' or 'Aphrodite', the Greek goddess of love.

DATES OF INTEREST

April 25. 1627
Company of New France, or The Hundred Associates, organized by Cardinal Richelieu. No Calvinist was allowed into New France. The de Caen Company Charter cancelled as they had failed to take out colonists.

April 25, 1849
Riots in Montreal, when Lord Elgin signed the Rebellion Losses Bill. His carriage was surrounded and escape was made to 'Monklands' by rapid driving. Mobs burned the House of Assembly, the public records of Upper and Lower Canada Parliaments and the records of the Parliament since the Union. He was stoned again five days later.

'Running into debt and long credits, have been the destruction of both property and religion among us'.

'The Letters of Mephibosheth Stepsure' by Thomas McCulloch, 1821.

Sir Charles Tupper's speech on the Canadian Pacific Railway was a masterly exposition and vindication of the Government railway policy. It can hardly fail to have a good effect, for Sir Charles said the Government is striving not only to develop the North West but to make all the provinces prosperous. *'Canadian Spectator', April 1882.*

Sir Charles Tupper. circa 1883.   The Public Archives of Canada

DID YOU KNOW THAT

In Newfoundland they 'sang' about taxes. These verses are from an anti-Confederation chant of the 1860's.

Cheap tea and molasses they say they will give,
All taxes take off that the poor man may live;
Cheap nails and cheap lumber our coffins to make,
And homespun to mend our old clothes when they break.

If they take off the taxes, how then will they meet
The heavy expense of the country's up-keep?
Just give them the chance to get us in the scrape,
And they'll chain us like slaves with pen, ink and red tape.

Would you barter the right that your fathers have won,
Your freedom transmitted from father to son?
For a few thousand dollars of Canadian gold
Don't let it be said that your birthright was sold.

Hurrah for our own native isle, Newfoundland!
Not a stranger shall hold one inch of its strand!
Her face turns to Britain, her back to the Gulf,
Come here at your peril, Canadian Wolf!

Here Lie the Remains of some of the Victims of the Frank Slide. April 29, 1903.

This inscription, on a common monument stone, is to the memory of the sixty-six persons who were killed in a landslide lasting only 100 seconds, when 90,000,000 tons of rock fell from Turtle Mountain in the Rockies on the small Alberta mining and railway community of Frank in the Crow's Nest Pass. A combination of geological faults, a small earthquake and coal-mining operations at the mountain base seem to have been responsible for the accident, that buried a square mile of the valley about forty-five feet. The C.P.R. westbound freight had just passed, and Sid Choquette, the brakeman, started back through falling rock to flag the on-coming 'Spokane Flyer'. The night shift of the Frank coal mine was leaving and found the entrance blocked tight. Thinking it a small cave-in, the men left by another exit to find their homes and families buried. Most perished instantly. The horses, left in the mine, all died.

APRIL

Have the autumn 1883 meeting of the British Association for Advancement of Science, in Toronto, instead of Ottawa... People do not want to be shut up in a lumber village with nothing to see. It would be injurious to have people return to England with such imperfect impressions of Canada as they would gain in Ottawa.

Toronto 'Evening Telegram', April, 1882.

Reply from 'The Ottawa Citizen', April 1882:

Toronto insolence! In keeping with the insolent tone of the grab-all spirit characterizing the Toronto press, Toronto selfishness is proverbial. The frequent display of it, by local papers, is not creditable to them.

McMaster University, Hamilton.   The Public Archives of Canada

OUR GRASS ROOTS

'Twelve Foot Davis', that colourful Albertan character, was not named for his size, for he stood only five foot five. In the 1849 gold rush, while prospecting in the Cariboo Creek area of British Columbia, he questioned the size of two staked claims. Finding they measured **twelve feet** too much, he staked the strip, making $20,000. Exceptionally industrious, he helped everybody, and died poor. All on the trail made for his cabin, for he was a tasty cook, famous for 'punkin pie'.

As he lay sick at Grouard, he said, 'Why should I be afraid to die? I never kilt nobody, I never stold from nobody, and I kept open house for travellers all my live. I ain't afraid to die.'

High over the Peace River that he loved is his tomb, with a stone shaped like a tree trunk, carrying this legend,

H. F. Davis, born Vermont 1820
Died Slave Lake, 1893
Pathfinder, Pioneer, Miner, Trader.
'He was everyman's friend
and never locked his cabin door'.

Dr. George W. Beers, a Montreal dentist, was known as the 'Father of Lacrosse'. In the middle 1860's, he framed a set of rules with the assistance of other Montreal sports enthusiasts.

DATES OF INTEREST

April 29, 1671
Royal letters patent approved establishment of the Sisters of the Congregation of Montreal (registered in Quebec, Oct. 17, 1672).

April, 1742
The son of La Vérendrye left Fort La Reine to explore country to the southwest in search of the Western Sea.

April, 1776
Benjamin Franklin, Chase, Carroll and Rev. John Carroll are sent to Montreal by American Congress to induce Canadians to rebel against Great Britain.

April, 1792
Capt. Geo. Vancouver sailed along the Pacific Coast from California, noting entrance of a 'small river', and passing the mouth of the Columbia as of no importance.

OLD TIMOTHY

'Seems as though we've alwuz had taxes, and mebbe we alwuz will, but no government yet has made us like it.'

April in the Hills

Today the world is wide and fair
With sunny fields of lucid air,
And waters dancing everywhere;
The snow is almost gone;
The noon is builded high with light,
And over heaven's liquid height,
In steady fleets serene and white,
The happy clouds go on.

I feel the tumult of new birth;
I waken with the wakening earth;
I match the bluebird in her mirth;
And wild with wind and sun,
A treasurer of immortal days,
I roam the glorious world with praise,
The hillsides and the woodland ways,
Till earth and I are one.

Archibald Lampman (1861-1899).

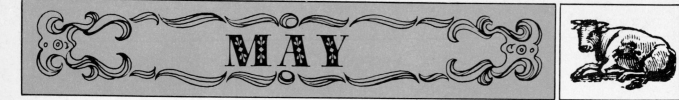

MAY

It was in 1872 that the shingle 'R. Simpson, Dry Goods' appeared at the corner of Queen and Yonge Sts., Toronto. In an era when the wholesaler was the Big Man of Business, a retail storekeeper was of little importance. Robert Simpson set out to change all that. He established the ritual of driving to his store each morning in great style, in an elegant victoria with a pair of fine horses. He was fashionably clad in a frock coat and high silk hat. Once having become known as a man of dignity, he exploded a bombshell that shocked Toronto — he had pictures of ladies' corsets in his advertisements.

The lily of the valley, the birthday flower for May, tells of purity, natural sweetness and humility. Many Canadians continue a custom brought from France, and on May first give a sprig of this lovely flower to friends as a good luck token.

*The young wheat is springing
All tender and green,
And the blackbird is singing
The branches between;
The leaves of the hawthorn
Have burst from their prison,
And the bright eyes of morn
On the earth have arisen.*

*Susanna Strickland Moodie,
about 1850.*

"Caravan en Route" by A. J. Miller.

The Public Archives of Canada

DID YOU KNOW THAT

All Indian tribes had one thing in common. From coast to coast they were inveterate gamblers, staking all on a game of chance – ornaments, clothing, canoes, pipes, weapons, and even wives. After the excitement of hunting and war, they filled the idle hours with gambling, smoking and dancing.

A favourite game used plum stones, or carved imitations, coloured white on one side and black on the other. Placed in a wooden bowl, which was struck sharply on the ground, these were sent into the air. The players bet on the colour that landed uppermost. Such gambling was often prescribed by the medicine man as a cure for the sick.

At times, neighbouring villages were challenged to a gambling session. Jean de Brébeuf, the Jesuit martyr, tells how the men of his village returned from a contest with another tribe. They were marching through snow several feet deep in bare feet for they had bet and lost their footgear, yet they were all in high good spirits.

Charles II of England signed a charter, May 2, 1670, granting to his first cousin Prince Rupert and his friends vast areas in America to be known as Rupert's Land. Thus the 'Gentlemen Adventurers of England trading into Hudson's Bay' received a rich monopoly, how rich no one then judged. Rupert's Land included the whole north from Labrador to the Rocky Mountains, where Winnipeg and Edmonton were some day to flourish, and beyond that territory even further north.

For this rich gift, Charles demanded nothing. True the monarch looked for a passage to Asia and his courtiers dreamed of precious gold, silver and gems, but there was no thought of settling the area, or of religious conversions.

Charles asked only as tribute, that on his sojourns in Rupert's Land he be presented with 'two black elks and two black beavers'. Creatures so rare were almost never found. Nor did King Charles' visit ever materialize.

However, history made everything right when King George VI and Queen Elizabeth, touring Canada in 1939, were presented with the fine skins, thus fulfilling the terms of the original charter.

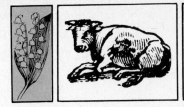

MAY

May 1, 1775
In Montreal, a bust of King George III, adorned with beads, cross and mitre and the words "Pope of Canada: Sot of England" was found. A reward of 500 guineas did not lead to the culprit.

May 1, 1822
Montreal General Hospital opened with accomodation for 80 patients.

May 2, 1602
Great hardship forced navigator George Weymouth back from his search for the Northwest Passage, losing the £500 promised by the East India Company. Chaplain John Cartwright had to return the robe given him to wear before the Great Khan, so sure was the Company of the passage to the east.

The statue of Queen Victoria, which may be seen in front of the Royal Victoria College, Montreal, was designed by her fourth daughter, H. R. H. Princess Louise, the wife of the Marquis of Lorne, Canada's Governor-General from 1878 – 1883.

1880 – Cure for Gout or Rumatick
Take two ounces of ungrount Brimstone and one ounce of salt peeter. Grind or pound them both together and mix them in one pint water and rub them to the part effected two times a day.

To Relieve Headache in Bed
If the head is much disturbed, wash it with cold water, and discontinue the night-cap; but wear worsted stockings in bed.

Circa 1780

Trees live longer than any other living thing, nor can they lie about their age. The botanist takes a thin core of wood from the tree and the annual rings that have been formed tell the true story.

Some trees have lived thousands of years. The Douglas firs and the western red and yellow cedars of British Columbia are the longest-living trees in Canada, and may live more than 1000 years. A Douglas Fir, felled at 1092 years, is thought to be the oldest in our Dominion. Not only do they grow to a great age, the Douglas Fir is also one of our largest trees. One towered 417 feet, with the first branch growing at 200 feet.

'Kamoose' Taylor, whose Hotel Macleod, Macleod, Alberta, was known all over the west in 1880, had very particular guest rules:

When guests find themselves or their luggage thrown over the fence, they may consider that they have received notice to quit.

Valuables will not be locked in the hotel safe. The hotel has no such ornament.

The bar will be open day and night. Day drinks, 50 cents; night drinks, $1.00. No mixed drinks will be served except in case of a death in the family.

Guests without baggage must sleep in the vacant lot, and board elsewhere until their luggage arrives.

Guests are forbidden to strike matches or spit on the ceiling, or to sleep in bed with their boots on.

Quarrelsome or boisterous persons, also those who shoot off without provocation guns or other explosive weapons on the premises, and all boarders who get killed, will not be allowed to remain in the house.

Crap, chuckluck, stud horse poker and blackjack are run by the management. Indians charged double.

OUR GRASS ROOTS

'Planting the Mai' was one of the happier customs of New France. Always eager for merriment and gaiety, the habitants placed a tree on the first day of May at the house of the Seigneur or Captain of Militia. Many voyageurs had returned from a winter's trading, loggers were back from the woods, and farmers welcomed the summer. All joined in trimming a tall tree, so that only a little greenery remained at the top. Festooned with garlands, this was put into place with song, music and dancing. Muskets were fired amidst cheers. Wine was passed and passed again. If the rougher men indulged in crude horseplay and tomfoolery, it was overlooked, and they, too, were invited to a breakfast as grand as the seigneur or captain was able to provide.

Newfoundland sayings.

An honest man when there's only anchors on the shore.

As salt as Lot's wife.

Many believe that it is lucky to carry a piece of hawthorn into the house during the first week in May.

OLD TIMOTHY

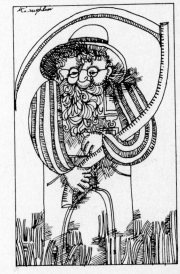

'I've met up with plenty of smart folks, but never met up with one yit who wuz smart in everythin'!'

Olsen, in 'Early Voyages and Northern Approaches', tells us that around 1000 A.D., the white falcon and polar bears from the Eastern Canadian Arctic were sent by the Kings of Norway as an impressive gift to other rulers.

In the 1840's buffalo herds roamed in vast numbers. During a hunt in the Red River area, 400 Indian and Métis hunters on ponies stampeded a herd, while others in the party killed 1300 animals in one day.

MAY

The 'Canadian Literary Magazine', 1833, says of John Galt, novelist and Commissioner of the Canada Company, 'He was the first to adopt the plan of opening roads before making a settlement, instead of leaving them to be cut by the settlers themselves — a plan which, under the irregular and patchwork system of settling the country then prevailing, has retarded the improvement of the Province more, perhaps, than any other cause.'

Galt, himself, was credited with this remark; 'Everybody who has been at Dover, Kent, England, knows it is one of the vilest hypochondriacal haunts on the face of the earth, except Little York in Upper Canada.'

May is said to derive its name from the mythological Maia, the goddess mother of Mercury, messenger of the gods. She was one of the seven daughters of Atlas, who carried the world on his shoulders.

Dr. Emily Howard Stowe, the first woman, in 1880, to practise medicine in Canada, had a daughter, Dr. Augusta Stowe-Gullen, who was first woman to graduate from a Canadian Medical School.

'I am a wife and mother and happy in my career'.

Madame Louis St. Laurent, wife of the former Prime Minister of Canada.

'When you take the child by the hand, you take the mother by the heart'.

An old Talmudic expression, heard in Wapella, Sask., where some twenty Jewish families settled on farms in 1886. John Heppner was the pioneer of the group.

The oldest continuing bookshop in Canada (1897), perhaps even in all of North America, is at 1011 St. John St., Quebec City. It is the only English book shop in the city, well supported by both French- and English-speaking Canadians.

RIEL'S COUNCILLORS IN 1885.

1. Johnny Sansregret.
2. Pierriche Parrenteau (a famous buffalo hunter).
3. Pierre Gariepy.
4. Philip Garnot, Secretary.
5. Albert Monkman.
6. Pierre Vandal.
7. Baptiste Vandal.
8. Toussaint Lucier (reputed to be the strongest man in the North-West).
9. Maxime Dubois.
10. Jimus Short.
11. — Touroud.
12. Emanuel Champagne.

Manitoba Archives.

The model for Uncle Tom in Harriet Beecher Stowe's 'Uncle Tom's Cabin' was Josiah Henson, a slave born in Port Tobacco, Maryland, in 1789. Threatened with separation from his wife and four children, he led them to Canada in 1830. The fugitives settled in Dresden, Ontario, near the Chatham terminus of the old underground railway that slaves rode to freedom. There Henson became pastor of a Negro church, established the Dawn Institute, a co-operative settlement of 100 ex-slaves, and started Henson's School, which anticipated by nearly three quarters of a century the first Canadian system of Technical Training. Rev. Josiah Henson died on May 18, 1883, at 94 at Dresden. His former home, on route 401, is pointed out as 'Uncle Tom's Cabin'.

When the board of governors of the University of Saskatchewan were searching for a campus site in 1908, they were wooed by Regina, Prince Albert, Moose Jaw, Battleford and, of course, Saskatoon. The story goes that one of the governors said, 'Moose Jaw! Moose Jaw! Now wouldn't that be an odd name for a college town?' 'Not at all', replied a proud native, 'What about Oxford?'

When John Buchan, Lord Tweedsmuir, pondered the call to the Governor-Generalship of Canada, 1935, he struggled very seriously with the knowledge that it would take him 'A week further away from Mother'.

OLD TIMOTHY

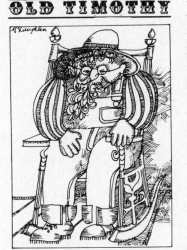

'In Newfunlan' when folks straighten out a mess, they say 'It's a good job outa a bad one'.'

The very names of our apples are beautiful – Golden Delicious, McIntosh Red, Winesap, Rome Beauty, Spartan, Crimson Beauty, Golden Russet, Melba, Nonpareil and Snow Fameuse. And did you know that the apple really belongs to the rose family?

'Stoup' was the old word for the verandahs of log cabins or frame houses. In an effort to make their first homes look a little nicer than the barns, the women grew morning glories to cover the stoup and hide the roughhewn logs.

'On approaching Montreal, the language and costumes . . . carried back our thoughts to Normandy and Brittany.'
Sir Charles Lyell, Scottish geologist, 1842.

The Indians have many other names for May. It is called Uye'kepesim, the Frog Moon, Sakepukawe-pesim, the Budding Moon or simply, the Planting Moon.

French Canadian farm women wore wooden shoes as late as the eighteenth century.

The lash was a frequent punishment in Quebec about 1759 for drunknness, selling liquor, or rioting, especially among British soldiers, who were given from 500 to 1000 strokes.

A deserter from the 10th Royal Veteran Battalion at Quebec, in 1810, received 450 strokes, and went to hospital to recover sufficiently to take the remaining 500 strokes of his sentence.

In 1809 a Montreal judge ordered 25 lashes on the bare backs of two dissolute women. The general public felt relieved when Canadian law abolished whipping of females in 1886.

One of the first extradition cases in the N. W. T. involved the Tebbitts couple, sought by Boston police in 1898 on an embezzlement charge. Mounties who boarded the train at Regina, correctly suspected the lady's fashionable bustle, and found it stuffed with bonds totalling $30,000.

'We will compel them to come in and accept this union, we will compel them by our fairness, our kindness, our love, to be one with us in this common and this great national work.'

Thomas D'Arcy McGee, House of Commons, 1868, on agitation in Nova Scotia for repeal of Confederation.

The rigours of the 1829 winter caused great suffering to the Scottish settlers of Megantic County, not too far from Thetford Mines, Quebec. During the first winter there was not one stove in the whole colony and it was almost as cold inside as out.

These strict Sabbath observers made it a rule that all water for Sunday be brought in on Saturday. As they had no wooden vessels, iron kettles and pots were used for the water, but the frost broke the receptacles. Finally the clergyman decided it would be better to bring the water in on Sunday than to chop ice on the Holy Day. When the church managed to get a stove, the congregation took turns sitting near it during the services. There is no record to show that the sermons were shortened.

Sir Samuel Cunard. Public Archives of Nova Scotia. Dalhousie University

OUR GRASS ROOTS

When Abraham Cunard emigrated with other struggling United Empire Loyalists to Nova Scotia, and found work in the Halifax Dock Yard, destiny was pointing the way. His son Samuel, born at the rear of what is now 257 Brunswick St., Halifax, in 1787, thought that 'steamers properly built and manned might start and arrive at their destination with the punctuality of railroad trains.' Yet in 1829 he wrote Ross and Primrose, Pictou, N.S. . . . 'We are entirely unacquainted with the cost of a steamboat, and would not embark in a business of which we are ignorant.'

Nevertheless, it took just eleven years for him to send the first Cunard ship across the Atlantic, the tiny 700 ton 'Unicorn', a wooden paddle steamer which left Liverpool on May 15, 1840, and reached Halifax on June 1 with 27 passengers.

'The situation in 1865 was so grave, in the opinion of the Canadian ministers, as to necessitate a conference with the Imperial government... It was, therefore, decided to send a delegation consisting of Macdonald, Cartier, Brown and Galt to discuss all these matters with the British cabinet... The following excerpts are from a letter which Alexander Tilloch Galt wrote his wife from London, May 17, 1865.

...The great event of Monday was our reception at Court. The morning was spent partly in arranging our uniforms. I had sent mine to the tailor's, to put it completely **en règle,** as you know the gold lace was not the correct width, and I had also to get the knee breeches, etc.... At a Court only those attend who are invited, and it is therefore a great distinction. Before the general reception began, the Queen ordered that we should be presented by Mr. Cardwell, as belonging to the Diplomatic circle, and that we should have the honour of kissing hands. Accordingly, we were ushered in, preceded by Mr. Cardwell, in the order of our seniority, Macdonald, Cartier, Brown and myself... The Queen looked very well, but little changed. She was dressed in black, with a long white veil attached to the back of her head. No ornaments, except a heavy pearl necklace... The Prince looked very well and has improved greatly since he was in Canada...

We all felt we had been treated with great distinction. Indeed our whole reception in England proves how important our mission is considered. We are treated quite as if we were ambassadors and not as mere Colonists as we have always been called.

We open our formal official communication on Friday, and hope a few days will settle things.'
The delegation resided at the Westminster Palace Hotel while in London.

On Sunday, divine service, according to the rites of the Church of England, will be in the Recollet's Church, and continue for the summer, beginning soon after eleven. The drum will beat each Sunday soon after half an hour past ten and the Recollet's bell will ring to give notice of the English service.
Quebec Gazette, 1767.

OUR GRASS ROOTS

Crocheted by the 80-year old Queen Victoria, in 1900, for heroes of the Boer War, seven khaki woollen scarves are held to be the world's rarest award for valour. Private Richard Rowland Thompson, of Ottawa, while serving with the Royal Canadian Regiment, was given the Queen's Scarf of Honour for rescuing wounded comrades. In one battle, he pressed his thumb on a comrade's jugular vein for seven hours and prevented him from bleeding to death.

Originally equal to the Victoria Cross, the Scarf has come to have even greater meaning. Given only to men in the ranks, the recipient was chosen by the soldiers themselves. This particular scarf recently turned up in Cork, Ireland, from where Thomson came. It was given to the Canadian War Museum, and will be placed in the New National Museum.

D. Sellers' Hotel, S.W. corner St. Clair and Yonge Sts. Toronto. 1855. The Public Archives of Canada.

DATES OF INTEREST

May 17, 1656
Dupuys and other Frenchmen left Quebec to form a settlement at Onondaga, at the request of the Indians of that name. The trip took them 2 months.

May 17, 1757
Four ounces of bread is the daily allowance in Quebec. Government contractors make large fortunes by increasing the price of bread from 3 to 30 sous per pound, and meat from 6 to 60 sous. Many Indians die of starvation and smallpox.

May 18, 1642
Maisonneuve landed on the Island of Montreal, and laid the foundations of the future city, calling the religious colony Ville-Marie.

May 18, 1677
Colbert wrote to Governor Frontenac, who was still quarreling with Intendant Duchesneau, exhorting him to live more amicably with him.

May 18, 1756
England declared war on France:

A western rancher suggests this cure for a bad cold – 'Put your hat on the table, drink well from a bottle of good whisky until you see two hats. Then get into bed, and stay there.'

'It may be a' vera fine; but it looks na' better to my thinken than hanks o' white woo' hung out o'er the bushes.' Spoken by a Scotch dragoon, on seeing the Montmorency Falls, Quebec, 1832.

'Roughing it in the Bush' by Susanna Moodie, 1852.

The Indians that Champlain met in the early 1600's had little regard for human life. They looked forward to 'a good hunting trip, plenty of sport, and the killing of many enemies before a happy return.'

MÅY

'Folks are friendlier in
Western Canada, where the pot
is alwuz boiling and the door is
alwuz on the latch.'

The Westminster Palace Hotel, London, England. The Illustrated London News 1860. The Public Archives of Canada.

**The English immigrants
used to say:**

'Eat sage in May
Live for aye'.

**In 1850, Toronto, with a
population of 30,000, had 152
taverns and 206 beer shops.**

The Talbot anniversary was a yearly fête instituted by John
Rolph honouring the day when his friend The Honourable
Thomas Talbot landed his canoe in Upper Canada. On May 21,
1830, the celebration was in the St. Thomas Hotel, in or near
Yarmouth Heights, when 'the prettiest girl in the district' led
off with the Colonel. She wore sky-blue poplin stripe (a blue
satin and a white stripe alternating) embossed, trimmed with
white satin and white blonde, white flowers and white gloves;
her shoes she made herself, getting the bootmaker to add fine
dancing soles.

DID YOU KNOW THAT

The affluent fur traders of the late 1700's lived in baronial
splendour in Montreal. Joseph Frobisher's 'Beaver Hall' was
famous for its hospitality. Every evening, carriages and calèches
brought the rich and important to his 80 by 36 foot log house,
overlooking lower Montreal and the St. Lawrence River. He
loved to give friends fine Guy and Bourassa apples from his
orchards with a view of Mount Royal.

Simon McTavish, known as 'Le Marquis', entertained as
lavishly in the imposing house which he had bought on St. Jean
Baptiste St. for his young bride, Marie Marguerite
Chaboillez.

After the struggles and dangers of wintering in the
wilderness, these fur traders surrounded themselves with every
luxury in a society that was truly bi-lingual to most, and
tri-lingual to some. (Their third language was often an Indian
dialect.)

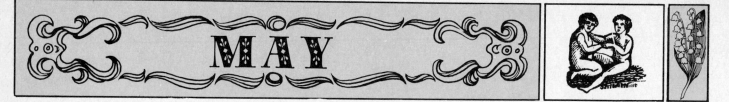

In 1799, David McCuen was granted a charter to ferry between Cornwall and St. Regis, specifying that he 'keep a sufficient boat, or batteau, and two good canoes.' A one-way trip was 2 shillings and sixpence.

By 1836, Ephraim Elliot advertised in the **Cornwall Observer** that he would run a 'Ferryboat from Barnhart Farm (2 miles above Cornwall) to Massena Point'. Rates were

Span of horses and wagon, $1.50
Yoke of Oxen, $1.00
Gig and Rider $1.00
Saddle-horse and Rider 75 cents
Foot Passenger 12¼ cents.

Stephen Leacock

In 1789, higher education in Canada began with the University of King's College, Windsor, N.S. A Royal Charter, granted by George IIII in 1802, proclaimed it 'the Mother of a University for the education and instruction of youth and students in Arts, to continue forever and to be called King's College.'

After destruction by fire in 1920, the University moved to Halifax, to the Dalhousie University Campus. A decade later, it entered into a partnership with Dalhousie, uniting the English and Scottish traditions.

Many Oxford customs continue. Faculty members function as 'dons' for the 'bays'. Donnish humour resulted in the naming of the bays – Chapel Bay is the furthest from the Chapel; Middle Bay is not in the middle; North Pole Bay, near the furnace, is the warmest and Radical Bay houses the theological students.

For the bride . . . The coiffure should be waved and rolled, and adorned with a bridal wreath and illusion veil, fastened at the throat, with a bouquet to match. *(1872)*

Jewellery was quite different in the 1800's. Ladies' watch chains were all of sixty inches long, wedding rings were wide and engraved with sentimental mottos, and jet was popular, for it took carving beautifully.

It was customary to wear black onyx or black enamel mourning rings, and brooches or lockets showing the departed one's hair under glass. Frequently a widower had a watch chain made of his deceased one's plaited hair, with gold tips and bands.

'If I were founding a university, I would found first a smoking room; then when I had a little more money in my hand, I would found a dormitory; then, after that, or more probably with it, a decent reading room and a library. After that, if I still had more money that I couldn't use, I would hire a professor, and get some text books.'
Stephen B. Leacock.

DID YOU KNOW THAT

Sir Henry Mill Pellatt was a man of brilliant and spectacular gifts. He made hundreds of sketches in Europe of chateaux from which E. J. Lennox designed the two million dollar Casa Loma 'Castle on the hill' in Toronto. Sumptuous within and without, Sir Henry and his family occupied it for little more than a decade. Known as a white elephant, it has become a convention centre and tourist mecca. Pellatt's career as a stock broker and financier was marked with dramatic incidents. An exceptional athlete, he won the amateur championship of America for the mile running race. He commanded the Queen's Own Rifles and in 1902 took the bugle band to England at his own expense to attend the coronation of King Edward VII. Eight years later, he defrayed the cost of taking the regiment to participate in the British Army Manoeuvres at Aldershot.

OUR GRASS ROOTS

'If you must preach go to Market Square', said the London, Ont., Chief of Police in May, 1882, as 19 year old Jack Addie and Joe Ludgate started the first open-air Salvation Army meeting in Canada. Market Square is still the Army's spot in London.

The evangelists were called 'The Devil Drivers', 'The Death and Glory Girls', 'Capt. Happy and His Hallelujah Wife' and 'Captain Glory', as they visited other provinces. On April 19, 1885, their message was 'General Booth sent us to fish on the Hallelujah line. In the taverns, theatres and gambling dens we will catch some drunkard here in Saint John, N.B:'

In 1886, a wire from Winnipeg to Toronto headquarters said 'Send more officers. Thermometer 30 degrees below. Salvation boiling over. The whole North West a blaze of salvation.'

On June 25, 1898, Salvationists covered the hazardous 548 miles from Skagway over the Chilkoot Pass to Dawson City where the rough prospectors contributed gold dust and nuggets.

The end of the century saw the Salvation Army from remote Newfoundland outports to British Columbia.

MAY

Even though 'Johnny Chinook' was quite a hunter, once he almost starved in the woods. Game was scarce, and he was down to his last bullet. He took careful aim at a flock of birds all on one branch – but missed. His bullet, however, split the branch and the two parts came together on the feet of all the birds.

Johnny was quite an angler too. They still tell of the 58 lb. pike he caught that had eight smaller fish inside, each weighing over 5 lbs.

Adopted children can cure warts or rashes by breathing on them.

To stop bleeding, turn the person's coat inside out, and a chair upside down.

Nova Scotians excel in recipes that call for molasses, for many prefer it to sugar as a sweetener. This stems back to the days when Bluenose vessels brought hogsheads of molasses from the West Indies. That, and rum!

For good luck, finish your spring cleaning before the end of May.
Quebec saying.

DATES OF INTEREST

May 24, 1892
Lacrosse game between Manitou and Morden in Manitoba. The C.P.R. put on a special excursion train when the Manitou team went to Winnipeg to play the 'Capitols' for the championship of Western Canada, and to win the silver cup.

May 24, 1918
Dominion gives Federal vote to women.

May 24, 1879
The 13th Regiment of Brooklyn, N.Y., with its chaplain, Rev. Henry Ward Beecher, came to Montreal to join the Canadian Militia in celebrating the Queen's Birthday. Rev. Beecher was the brother of Harriet Beecher Stowe, author of 'Uncle Tom's Cabin'.

May 27, 1755
'When with Whale Boats Crue to ye Gut and Bought a mess of cold fish of ye French. Dined at a Tavern thare. Some Rany.'

From an officer at Annapolis Royal Basin with the forces of Lieut. Col. Winslow.

Indian Salvation Army. Fort Simpson.   *The Public Archives of Canada.*

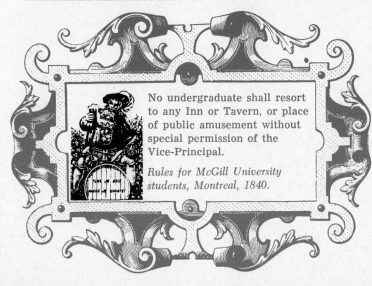

No undergraduate shall resort to any Inn or Tavern, or place of public amusement without special permission of the Vice-Principal.

Rules for McGill University students, Montreal, 1840.

'The 24th of May had been dedicated to Queen Victoria, and called Victoria Day; it was also a public holiday. English Canadians welcomed it with enthusiasm; French Canadians did not like, even symbolically, to bow the knee before an English Queen. But they wanted a holiday. So they found a compromise – they kept the holiday on May 24 and called it Dollard Day.'
Professor E. R. Adair.

No object tends more to the furtherance of a young Colony than its Roads, particularly in a severe northern Climate. Much has been said – little done. Since annual improvements extend over the wilderness of our Island, we congratulate the Colony on the melioration.

They like old things in Nova Scotia, and have many that are historically important. One of the most cherished is a flag, designed from the royal coat-of-arms granted the province in 1625. This ensign dates to 1621 when King James I of England granted a charter to William Alexander. It shows a blue St. Andrew's Cross on white, with a gold lion of Scotland.

JUNE

OUR GRASS ROOTS

The story goes that the Fathers of Confederation were having quite a time deciding what Canada should be called, back in 1867. Sir Leonard Tilley, one of the committee studying this problem, opened his Bible at verse 8 of the 72nd Psalm, 'He shall have dominion from sea to sea and from the river unto the ends of the earth.'

He told the other committee members of this, and the aptness of the phrase influenced them in the decision to adopt the name 'Dominion of Canada'.

Hon. Sir Samuel Leonard Tilley.   *The Public Archives of Canada.*

The 'Bees' were just about the only form of social entertainment in early days. There was plenty of whiskey, for this Canadian nectar was only 50 cents a gallon, and enormous quantities of food were served. It was nothing for the hostess to cook up a peck or more of potatoes, and place huge joints of salt pork on the table. All worked together, the high born mingling with the low. There were 'Bees' of every variety such as husking, chopping, raising, moving, logging, settling, sugaring, spinning, quilting, roofing and others as the need arose.

The astrolabe bearing the date 1603, used by the incredibly brilliant navigator, explorer and King's Geographer, Samuel de Champlain, was lost on June 7, 1613 on one of his early voyages. After two and a half centuries, it was found again in 1867, the year that Canada became a nation, by a fourteen year old wood cutter. It is now the property of the New York Historical Society, and displayed at the museum at 170 Central Park West.

A cairn near highway 17 up Cobden way, Ontario, marks the spot where this important find was made.

The rose is the birthday flower for June. The red rose speaks of love; the white of purity and silence; and the yellow denotes jealousy.

DATES OF INTEREST

June 1, 1876
'The Old Eighteen' was the popular term for the first cadets at Royal Military College, Kingston, which opened on this date.

June 2, 1824
Mrs. Judge (Samuel) Anderson, died, aged 81.

June, 1836
Judge Anderson died, aged 99 or 100.

June 5, 1755
Obeying a proclamation, 418 Acadian men met in church at Grand Pré, N.S., when Col. Winslow read 'His Majesty's final resolution – that your lands and tenements, cattle and live stock are forfeited to the Crown with all effects, saving money and household goods.'

June 6, 1898
At the time of the Gold Rush, a two-weeks old newspaper arrived in Dawson from Seattle 'outside'. Crowds of men paid a dollar each for standing room while the paper was read aloud.

June 8, 1824
Noah Cushing, of Quebec, received the first patent issued by Canada – for a washing and fulling machine.

'Put to the torture ordinary and extraordinary' – June 6, 1752.

The tall Calvary seen above the fence of the Grey Nunnery, Guy and Doorchester Blvd., Montreal, reminds antiquarians of a sinister 'on the spot' murder and the horrible fate of the criminal. In 1752, when but a few thousand French colonists lived between St. James St., and the St. Lawrence River, Jean Favré and his wife were murdered by a neighbour, Jean Baptiste Goyer dit Bélisle, also a farmer. Bélisle had protected himself with an airtight alibi, which however failed him when he talked foolishly in taverns. He was convicted of the foul deed, of which he boasted while drunk.

An extract from the 'Requisition of the King's Attorney, done at Montreal, this 6th June, 1752' reads . . . 'Bélisle be condemned to have arms, legs, thighs, and backbone broken, he alive, on a scaffold in the market-place (where the Customs House stands on Youville Square); then on a rack, his face to the sky, he be left to die. Previously put to the torture ordinary and extraordinary, his body shall be carried to the highway'. This wretched event was marked by a tall red cross, which the good Grey Sisters painted afresh each year until 1948 when it was replaced by the present Calvary.

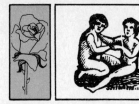 

OLD TIMOTHY

'In pioneer times, the bride in Acadia usta show she could weave homespun — the groom that he could make wooden wheels.'

June boasts three fascinating gems as birthstones: pearls, moonstones and alexandrites. The moonstone is considered a happy and lucky stone, and a symbol of friendship. The alexandrite tells of mystery.

June is supposed to have taken its name from the 'Juniores' or juniors, of Rome, or from the goddess Juno, wife of Jupiter, the king of the Roman gods of mythology.

'If the mills of God grind slowly, the mills of Parliament sometimes seem to stop altogether – that is, of course, so far as great fundamentals are concerned.'
From a 1928 speech by the famous Albertan Dr. Irene Parlby, the second woman cabinet minister in the British Commonwealth.

The first wedding in the High River community of the N.W.T. took place in 1886 between Duncan Fraser and Jessie Spalding. Their son, Jack, was the first white child born in High River.

30,000 head of cattle of the Powder River Cattle Company, formed in 1882, were frozen to death or starved in two winters.
'Nor-West Farmer', June 1888.

There were fewer than twenty divorces in Canada in any year prior to 1900.

DID YOU KNOW THAT

Tom Longboat, (Cog-Wa-Gee) who was born on June 4, 1887 on the Six Nations Reserve near Brantford, Ont., became the champion long-distance runner in America.
With odds of 100 to 1, he won the Hamilton City 'Around the Bay' race in 1906; beat a horse over a 12 mile course; won the 15 mile Toronto Marathon in three successive years; and ran 60 miles to enlist with the 180th Sportsmen's Battalion. Always unmanageable, he was spoken of as the most difficult recruit to train in the whole British Empire. His reply was 'The time has come for a married man to enlist'.
'The swiftest of his race since Deerfoot'.

Tom Longboat.   The Public Archives of Canada.

'We would like you to keep to the Standard, that Mr. Radisson agreed to, but withall to give the Indians all manner of Content and Satisfaction'.
Letter to Governor Geyer, Port Nelson, from the Governor and Committee of Hudson's Bay Company, London, June 2, 1688.

A sense of adventure brought many Jewish pioneers to British Columbia at the time of the gold strike. After the excitement of the stampede, a great many stayed on in Victoria, so that by 1863 there were enough to build a synagogue. 'The whole affair was a sort of gala occurrence. The band of H.M.S. Topaz came from Esquimault to take part in the ceremony. The members of the Hebrew Congregation were met in open procession by the Germania Sing Verein, the French Benevolent Society, St. Andrew's Society, Masonic Lodges, Fraternal Societies, officers and others, who marched in parade to the site where the cornerstone was to be laid . . .
'Who would have thought,' said Samuel Hoffman, 'that in the short space of five years we should have a temple erected where aboriginies were then lords of the dominion?'
'The British Colonist', Victoria, B.C., June, 1863.

Some say Bluenose is a nickname applied to Nova Scotians and New Brunswickers by the 19th century humourist, Justice Thomas Chandler Haliburton. An explanation has it that after 1840, Canadian ship-owners operated a vast number of Maritime-built vessels. Sailing home from the West Indies, loaded with sugar and rum, the captains battled a bitter cold nor'west wind and took what comfort they could from the rum. The fierce wind and the rum turned their noses blue, hence they were called the Bluenose skippers. Still another source says the name comes from the wonderful Bluenose potato of the Maritimes, which takes a blue colour in the light.

When King George VI and Queen Elizabeth visited Regina in June 1939, the City Fathers planned an exclusive function in their honour. Lieutenant-Governor Archibald Peter McNab said, 'Nothin' doin'! Only a few could attend. I want every man, woman and child to see the King and Queen.' As 10,000 children cheered on the Parliament Grounds, Archie turned to the Queen and said, 'My! My! It's too bad you didn't bring the kids!'

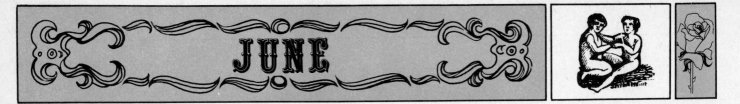

The well-to-do ladies of Upper and Lower Canada liked to wear little lace point collars, often 'from home' which cost anywhere from twenty dollars up. The exquisite piece was worn fastened with an heirloom brooch, treasured because of associations with the old country.

OLD TIMOTHY

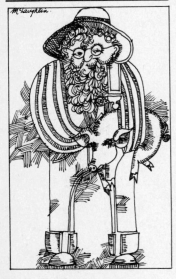

'The homesteaders called it a society wedding when the bride wore white and the groom shaved.'

In the North-west, the Chipewyan Indians placed their dead in the trees. Of this custom, a brave said, 'You white men live on things that grow on the ground and bury your dead in the ground, which is right for you. Indians, like us, live on things that run above ground, and want to take our last sleep above in the trees.'

Out West, it was generally believed that even a wild horse would not hurt a drunken man.

In Newfoundland, the purplish pitcher plant (Sarracenia purpurea), which had been suggested for use on the coinage by Queen Victoria, was made an official emblem in June 1954. It is also called Indian dipper and the Huntsman's cup.

Altho York is under 2000 souls, there are 60 taverns in which strong beer or spiritous liquors are sold or drank at all hours, day or night. Many are creditably kept, but others, the resort of the idle, the dissipated and the profligate are known to the magistrates, and in some cases owned by them.

'Colonial Advocate', June 12, 1828.

June is still the favoured month for weddings, and despite population explosions, threats of famine, and the pill, most brides will adorn themselves with orange blossoms for luck.

Do they know that the orange is a prolific plant whose tender flowers denote fertility?

The steamer **Bonanza King** came proudly into port from Lake Labarge. Originally for White Horse Rapids, she went to the wrecked **Domville**. At Thirty Mile River, she took on the **Domville's** 25 passengers, 70 tons of freight, 500 sheep, and 1500 lbs. of fine trout and whitefish for the Dawson market. At Fort Selkirk, she hooked on a tow barge of 85,000 feet of lumber, which drew six inches more water than the **Bonanza King** herself.

The steamer **Ora**, the first boat from the outside, pulled into Dawson, four days out of White Horse.

'Klondike Nugget', Dawson, N.W.T. June 17, 1899.

Steamer Bonanza King leaving Dawson. In her cargo there is $.2,000,000 in gold. The Public Archives of Canada.

DID YOU KNOW THAT

There is a painting in the Archives of Canada, at Ottawa, showing the arrival towards the end of the 17th century of 'The King's Daughters' at Quebec, with the men, eager to choose a bride, lined up in their best finery, watching the girls disembark. Each newly-married couple was given 'THE KING'S GIFT', a dowry which consisted of one ox, one cow, a pair of swine, a pair of fowl, two barrels of salted meat, and eleven crowns. Intendant Jean Baptiste Talon, of New France, often added a horse. Land to be cleared was easily found at one of the seigneuries along the St. Lawrence River or the Richelieu River. These farms were virtually forts, as a protection against the Indians.

'Paper Bread', Old Indian and Métis Recipe.

Take 3 or 4 handfuls of corn meal and a little salt. Add enough water to make a gruel. Cook until like porridge. Heat a very big flat rock, on your open fire. The rock must be hot enough to make a drop of water fly off. Take some of the dough in your hand, and quickly wipe it across the rock. It cooks right away, so peel it off when it ruffles on the edges. The best paper bread is very thin.

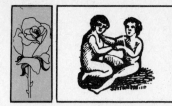

JUNE

The Fathers of Confederation averaged 46 years of age. Four were in their thirties and over half were fortyish.

Indian names for June are The Rose Moon and Opinayawa' wepesim, The Egg-Laying Moon.

The ladies of New France, mothers and daughters alike, were mad for aigrettes. This was the best of all gifts that could be brought them from Europe. Vain, and extremely fond of elaborate hair-dos, for street as well as salon, the lucky girl with an aigrette was hard put not to wear it on every occasion.

Montreal passed through many stages. The birch bark tents were followed by a whole camp of all sorts of tents, before it became an outpost and then a frontier town. In 1642 all the houses were of wood.

What do you call the mischievous Canada jay? From Newfoundland to British Columbia, this cheerful bird goes by many names, so choose from whisky jack, lumberjack, whisky john, moose bird or meat hawk.

Prime Minister King led his Liberal Party back into office for the third time in ten years, but the overwhelming Liberal preponderance was slashed to a bare majority on the civilian vote count.

Montreal Star, June 12, 1945.

In 1946, as a gift of gratitude, Queen Juliana sent 20,000 bulbs to Ottawa, where her youngest daughter was born, thus starting the Tulip Festival.

Mrs. Norquay, wife of the Hon. John Norquay, Premier of Manitoba from 1878 to 1888, told of her marriage in 1862 at Portage La Prairie:

'Marriages, held before noon on Wednesdays, were followed by three days' dancing. On Sunday the newly-wedded couple went to church together . . . We lived on fish when the grasshoppers ate everything green. Salt was scarce. Meat was dried, not salted. We dried raspberries, saskatoons and blueberries in a cake, and broke off a piece as needed. We put pounded choke cherries with the pemmican just as currant jelly with mutton'.

View of Montreal, from a sculptured relief. The Public Archives of Canada.

OUR GRASS ROOTS

In the Huron Tract in the 1825-50 period, one parson held 'wood-shed weddings' to discourage couples from finding him at his own house, as there his fee was but one dollar. By meeting them at a hotel, in their own homes, or elsewhere, he was entitled to collect five dollars.

Canadian patents granted between June 1824 and Sept. 1872 reveal how our society developed. The following were chosen from 5,000 issued in those 48 years: A gauge to ascertain the tonnage of goods shipped on canal boats; a new and useful invention for preparing lamps for producing light similar to gas; a machine for extracting stumps from new lands; a new machine, hung with nets, for taking eels; a plan for the turning of 4-wheel carriages in a short space; a limited horse swing; a new shape of bar iron for horse shoes; new yokes for oxen; a useful process of manufacturing leather from the skin of the whale or porpoise; a metallic burial case and an invention for propelling boats against the wind and in all directions with the same wind.

Those subject to sore throat should bathe the neck in cold water in the morning, and use the flesh-brush at night, which will be found to relieve them very much.

'1865 Almanac and Register', New Brunswick.

DATES OF INTEREST

June 10, 1611
Biard and Massé, Jesuits, wrote the first letters sent to France from New France.

June 10, 1611
Henry Hudson and son set adrift in Hudson's Bay by his mutinous crew.

June 11, 1776
American Order of the Day, at Sorel: 'Every non-commissioned officer or soldier come to parade dirty, with a long beard, or his breeches knees open, shall be mulcted of a day's allowance of provision, and do a double tour of duty.'

June 12, 1811
In the Red River district, the Earl of Selkirk purchased 116,000 square miles of land from The Hudson's Bay Company at a price of ten shillings.

June 13, 1886
Vancouver, pop. about 2,000, was almost entirely razed by fire, the year it was incorporated.

June 13, 1776
Arnold, at Montreal, wrote 'The junction of the Canadas with the colonies is at an end. Let us quit them and secure our own country before it is too late.'

June 16, 1659
The King of France began to aid emigrants to Canada.

June 16, 1898
First issue of 'Klondike Nugget', Dawson, N.W.T. When Eugene Allen started this paper, it was fifty cents an issue.

JUNE

The Fire at St. John. The Illustrated London News. 1877.

The Public Archives of Canada.

DATES OF INTEREST

June 19, 1644
The Mohawk council decided to let Jesuit missionary Bressani live and gave him to one of their old women to replace a deceased relative. As the Iroquois had tortured and mangled him cruelly, she thought him useless and sold him to the Dutch, who gave him passage to France.

June 20, 1877
Saint John, N.B. was more than two thirds destroyed by a fire, which burned every church and store. 1600 homes were razed, leaving 13,000 without shelter. The loss was $27,000,000. Fire was not new to Saint John for in earlier years shipyards, wharves, vessels and homes had been devastated by fierce blazes.

June 22, 1774
The Quebec Act, which received royal assent, decreed that the Custom of Paris was to be continued in disputes relative to property and civil rights, but in criminal matters the law of England was to hold.

In Upper Canada, settlers produced a lemonade-like drink by steeping 'the flowers of the sumach' in boiling water.

The origin of the name Acadie goes back many years for the word is found in the Micmac Indian tongue. Gestaldi's map of 1584 shows the area as Larcadie, but after 1604, it was known as Acadie. Explorers Cabot (1497), Juan Alvarez (1520), Jean Verrazano (1524), Estevan Gomez (1524-5) and Jacques Cartier (1534) all seem to have noted the spot.

JAMES LEY,
ELLESMERE,
Manufacturer of
CARRIAGES, WAGONS, CUTTERS, SLEIGHS,
And Agricultural Implements,
Special attention to the making and repairing of Iron and Wrought Beam Ploughs, Horse Shoeing, etc.,
Wood Work furnished by T. R. ALLISON, ELLESMERE.

Isaac Armstrong,

Contractor and Builder,

And General Carpenter.

LOT 33, CON. D. SCARBORO.

DID YOU KNOW THAT

The destinies of the French settlers in Acadia of 1604-5 were shaped by the Franco-British struggles for colonial power. There were offences on both sides. Matters boiled when British soldiers were massacred in Grand Pré and Charles Lawrence, the British governor of Nova Scotia, expelled the Acadians in 1755, in what their descendants still remember as a 'tragedy without equal'.

Unofficial figures claim that over 5000 men, women and children were deported. Two shiploads reached France but were refused permission to land, and then settled along the Atlantic American sea-board. A caravan of over 700, still spoken of as 'The Heroic Ones', walked 600 miles through forest land to make new homes in what is now New Brunswick.

Many made their way to Louisiana, where they were called Cajuns, an easy name transition.

During their wanderings, they seldom saw a priest, so few unions were church-sanctioned. In later years, a Nova Scotia parish register bears this entry by the priest, "Today, I married a couple in the presence of their grown children.'

It was a unique June wedding. It took over 100 yards of white satin and lace and large clusters of orange blossoms to adorn the bride, Anna Swan, the 22 year old, 7½ foot, 350 lb. giantess from Nova Scotia. Her bridegroom was an even taller and heftier Kentucky giant.

They dwarfed the minister, a six foot three Nova Scotian, who married them at St. Martin-in-the-Fields, London, on June 17, 1871. The bride wore a diamond ring, given her by Queen Victoria before whom the couple had performed. As 'the largest married couple in the world' they were on exhibition at $1000 per month. Their two children died as infants.

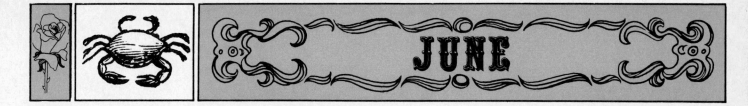

JUNE

Charlottetown, circa 1843.

The Public Archives of Canada.

OUR GRASS ROOTS

Remember how Canada started? There were meetings from 1864 to 1867 in Quebec, Halifax, St. John and Charlottetown. Then the British North America Act gave us Confederation, 1867, uniting Ontario, Quebec, Nova Scotia and New Brunswick, with provisions for others to join when ready.

Sir John A. Macdonald said, 'We must have some form of colonial unity. We seek to found a great land . . . we must seek it now.'

The 'Big Three' Fathers of Confederation were Sir John A. Macdonald, the Architect of the Dominion; his bitter enemy, George Brown, founder and publisher of the **Toronto Globe**; and Sir George Etienne Cartier. Unlike the other two, Brown refused a knighthood, wishing to remain free in his editorial policy.

Although Prince Edward Island has been immortalized as the 'Cradle of Confederation', it did not join until 1873.

After eighty-two years, the entry of our tenth province, Newfoundland, in 1949, united Canada within Confederation.

The first two bishops of Montreal had their headquarters in historic St. Jacques Church, St. Denis and Ste. Catherine Sts., which was built in 1823, and which almost a century and a half later became the bilingual Roman Catholic Church for Expo '67. Because of the nearby subway station, that moves about 20,000 people daily, fifteen masses are celebrated on Sundays, alternating between English and French. The present structure is the fourth on the same site, all bearing the same name, and each built when the previous one had been destroyed by fire.

If you find a white button, good luck will be yours for sure. That's what they say in Newfoundland, where other good luck omens are spying two black crows overhead, hearing a rooster crow at one's doorstep, dreaming of one's father and seeing a sleeping baby smile.

The student of toponomy (the nomenclature of places) will find the derivation of Toslow, Newfoundland, worth a thought. This little fishing village of long ago took its name from Tasse de l'Argent (cup of silver), through Toslow John to its present name.

'If the cows run home in the evening with their tails straight out behind them, it's a sure sign of rain. If their tails are down, we can prepare for a fine day.'

This hint is from the weather-wise Mennonites of Manitoba, Alberta and Saskatchewan.

OLD TIMOTHY

'The feller on the next quarter-section don't havta tell me what he believes, I kin see how he lives.'

'Civility is a cheap coin that . . . goes further than dollars and cents.'

'The Clockmaker, or The Sayings and Doings of Samuel Slick, of Slickville' by Justice Thomas Chandler Haliburton, 1836.

JUNE

Eight million sightseers annually visit Niagara Falls, the seventh natural world wonder. The world's honeymoon capital attracts not only lovers but odd stunt artists. Many have died going over the falls on a tight rope, in barrels, rubber balls, rafts and boats, swimming and leaping.

On June 30, 1859, 25,000 watched the daring Monsieur Blondin, 'The Prince of Manila', walk a tight rope to the Canadian side, stopping to drink champagne and to turn a back somersault. Later, his rope 'novelties' included blindfolding, riding a bicycle, pushing a wheelbarrow, standing on his head, crossing at night and, finally, carrying his manager piggyback.

One of the very oldest churches in Acadia is on the Island La Vallière. For reasons now lost in antiquity (the church dates from 1679), the burial place was laid out across the river. From this stems the long established custom of arranging all funerals at low tide.

DATES OF INTEREST

June 24, 1813
Laura Secord, the Loyalist heroine of the War of 1812-14, walked some twenty miles through swamp and forest of enemy – held land to warn Lieut. James FitzGibbon of a surprise attack from the Americans at Beaver Dam. She had discovered this project from American troops billeted in her house at Queenston.

June 26, 1857
Two steamboats left Quebec for Montreal — the **Napoleon** and the **Montreal.** At Cap Rouge, fire broke out on the **Montreal** and although the **Napoleon** steamed to the rescue, 253 lives were lost in fifteen minutes. The St. Andrew's Society took charge, paying for the tragic burials in the Mount Royal Cemetery, Montreal. A month later the Grand Jury, at Quebec, reported bills for manslaughter against the owner and officers of the **Montreal.**

June 28, 1867
Annual meeting of Quakers constituted.

June 28, 1886
The first Canadian Pacific Railway passenger train left Montreal and arrived at Vancouver on July 4, running 2906 miles in 140 hours.

June 29, 1786
Depopulating almost a whole parish, a band of 526 immigrants from Loch Nevis, west Highlands of Scotland, sailed with their priest, Rev. Alexander Macdonnell, on the ship 'McDonald', reaching Quebec Sept. 7. (70 days). Arriving in Glengarry, they built a Roman Catholic Church, known as 'The Blue Chapel'.

June 29, 1850
Coal was discovered on Vancouver Island.

Niagara Falls.   circa 1859.

OUR GRASS ROOTS

Edouard Beaupré, the giant from southern Saskatchewan, stood 8 ft. 2½ inches, as against the 7 ft. 9 inch stature of Angus MacAskill from Cape Breton. But Angus weighed more. He tipped the scales at 700 lbs. while the ranchboy weighed only 396 lbs. Possibly Edouard had not yet really filled out, for he was just a growing boy and 17 years younger than Angus when these comparisons were made.

In a province where people just about lived in the saddle, things became rough for the towering young lad, for even mounted on the tallest horse, his feet trailed the dust.

Clothes were a problem. It took a good-sized buck to supply the makings for deerskin moccasins for his size 25 feet and two dozen yards of cloth for a suit.

He toured with a circus, often appearing with Louis Cyr, the strong man from Quebec. Like Cyr he performed many stunts with horses. The crowds always cheered when he picked up a 700 pound steed with one hand and held it shoulder high.

In spite of his size and strength, his career was short. While on tour, a bad cold developed into pneumonia, and caused his untimely death at 21, in 1904.

'For six or eight inches of rolled tobacco, we got (from the Indians) sturgeons weighing, the bones being taken out, twenty to thirty pounds. Indians . . . seldom thank one, only . . . grunt satisfaction.'

John Lefroy, Lake Winnipeg, June 28, 1843, on the journey from Fort William to Fort Garry.

Before 1763:

The first bath of the season in French Canada was frequently taken on St. Jean Baptiste Day in the waters of a river.

The June 24th holiday of French Canada, with its fleur-de-lis flag, is still observed with a bonfire ceremony, even as in 1636 when New France had but 200 colonists. The one-day celebration is now a week-long holiday, and the bonfires blaze from Gaspé to Montreal, along the St. Lawrence River.

The St. Jean Baptiste Societies, formed in Montreal in 1834 and in Quebec in 1842, mark the occasion with magnificent torch-light processions, serious cultural presentations and informal singing and dancing in the streets. In Montreal, a four and a half mile kaleidoscopic parade offers towering symbolic figures, bands and floats.

Sir William Van Horne, of the Canadian Pacific Railway, was ahead of his time in many ways. He had a real flair for advertising and publicity, for there was nothing of the shrinking violet in his personality. When he was proud of something, he said so. The day the new Windsor Station opened in Montreal, his ads proclaimed,

'Beats all creation
That C.P.R. station.'

OLD TIMOTHY

'Wuz an ole-timer in Calagry usta say kissin' girls is a bad habit. Like eatin' soup with a fork, ye never git enuff.'

Arrival in Vancouver of the first C.P.R. transcontinental train. The Public Archives of Canada.

DID YOU KNOW THAT

William Dunlop, Warden of the Forests of the Canada Company, Upper Canada, author and surgeon, had a style all his own. At a time when social correspondence was verbose and flowery, his answer to a dinner invitation was 'I'll come'. When this man, known as 'The Tiger', 'The Doctor' and 'The Backwoodsman', died June 28, 1848, his will said, in part:

'I leave ... property to my sisters, Helen Boyle Story and Elizabeth Boyle Dunlop; the former because she is married to a minister whom (God help him) she henpecks. The latter because she is married to nobody, nor is she like to be, for she is an old maid and not market-rife.... I leave Parson Chevasse (Magg's husband) the snuff-box I got from the Sarnia Militia, as ... gratitude for taking a sister that no man of taste would have taken. I leave John Caddle a silver teapot, to the end that he may drink tea there from to comfort him under the affliction of a slatternly wife ... I leave my sister Janet my Granma's snuff mull, as it looks decent to see an old woman taking snuff.'

The voyageurs learned from the Indians to offer a bit of tobacco to the spirit of the angry rivers during a storm, for the natives considered tobacco to be 'strong medicine' in their culture. The smoke of the tobacco took thoughts and prayers to the gods, and messages to those afar. No treaty was binding unless sealed by the smoking of the calumet or ceremonial pipe.

Learning from the Indians, the French Canadians in New France had excellent tobacco crops. However, pressure was exercised by the priests who wanted them to switch to other crops, as tobacco was not subject to church tithes.

To cure those sick with fever, Indians placed them in 'Sweating Huts'. The enclosure became filled with steam when they threw water over red-hot stones. Those who were healthy spent time in the sweat bath, too, for it had religious significance. It was felt that the invocations which accompanied the steam rituals insured tribal successes in future endeavours.

The hut was usually built near a body of water and summer or winter, after a session in the hot vapour, the Indians jumped into the lake for a swim.

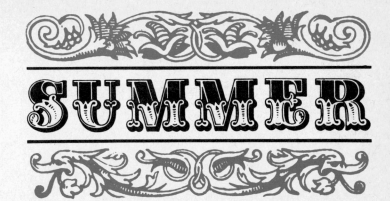

SUMMER

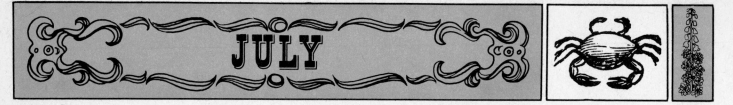

JULY

Scarcely had the sound of rejoicing . . . upon the celebration of Dominion Day passed away, when (we) were again called upon to join with the citizens of the Great Republic to celebrate the 92nd anniversary of their independence. . . . At sunrise and at noon salutes were fired; and people gathered to hear the Declaration of Independence read . . . The reading and speeches were interspersed with national airs of the United States, and closed with 'God Save the Queen'.

'Cariboo Sentinel', Barkerville, B.C. July 4, 1868.

DID YOU KNOW THAT

Lady Macdonald saw the Canadian Rockies in a highly unorthodox manner in July 1886, while travelling with the Prime Minister on the new Canadian Pacific Railway, which had been completed eight months before. This adventurous lady rode on the 'scoop' or 'cow catcher' of the locomotive, enjoying an intimate view of the pass of the Kicking Horse River and the valleys of the Columbia and Fraser Rivers.

The mosquitoes were now (July 5, 1892) thick beyond anything. Hunting became impossible, their stings could not be endured, and in looking through such dense swarms, it was not possible to take sure sight. This part of the Yukon (foot of the Canyon) is scarcely habitable in the summer, on account of these pests, reason for the complete absence of game at that time. At the first severe frost, about September first, this annoyance is abated completely.   Canadian *Magazine*, 1893.

In the hearts and minds of the delegates who assembled in this room on Sept. 1, 1864 was born the Dominion of Canada.

'Providence being their guide They builded better than they knew.'
Inscription on plaque erected 1917, in the Legislative chamber, Charlottetown, P.E.I.

Melt small pieces of common soap in a vessel placed in a pan over the fire. Add an equal quantity of coarse sand sifted from the very coarsest, keep over fire until the sand is as hot as the soap. Pour into a cup or mould, keeping hot by means of hot water until the mixture is completely pressed into a mass. When hard, this washball rubbed with warm water, against corns or callous heels, will render them quite soft and easy.
The COOK Not Mad, or, Rational Cookery'. **Cooking without food, 1832.**

The early settlers suffered many food shortages. Susanna Moodie tells of substitute dishes, made of 'Nothing'. Dandelions were blanched to a cream colour and used as salad 'quite equal to endive' or boiled with pork instead of cabbage. The roots made good coffee, and the tops excellent beer. Squirrels were used as roasts and in pies and stews. The black squirrel was deemed very palatable. The lake was their 'Pantry' and they used bass, eel, white fish, salmon, and maskinonge in stews, soups, and pies. Huckleberries, gooseberries, cranberries, blackberries, wild cherries and currants abounded.

A little boy walked straight to his teacher on his first day at school, and said 'Well, lick me and let me go to my seat.'

Teacher, 'Do you know why I am going to whip you?'
Boy, 'Yes, because you're bigger'n I am.'

'Who made you?' asked a primary teacher.
Child, 'God made me so long,' indicating the length of a small baby, 'and I growed the rest.'

'What are the chief imports of Canada?'
'Immigrants'.
'Humor in the School-Room,' by James L. Hughes, Inspector of Public Schools, Toronto, from the 'Canadian Magazine', July, 1893.

OLD TIMOTHY

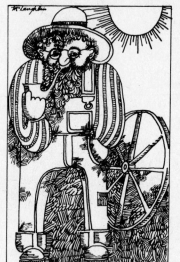

'Knew an ole sodbuster usta say ev'ry mountain makes at least two valleys'.

To cure styes on the eyes, rub with grandmother's gold wedding ring.

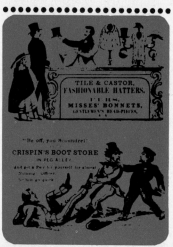

DATES OF INTEREST

July 1, 1924
A Stampede Celebration marked the 50th anniversary of the building of Fort Macleod, as the headquarters of the North-West Police. Mounties led the parade, followed by men of the N.W.M.P. of 1874. The area was crowded with 15,000 people: Indians in tribal regalia, cowboys, statesmen, and ranchers.

July 2, 1578
Sir Martin Frobisher, pioneer explorer seeking the Northwest passage, was sure he would also find gold west of Greenland. They 'sawe so much yce, that we thought it vnpossible to get into the Streightes; yet at the last we gaue the adventure, and entered the yce . . . looking eurie houre for death'. It was a 'dismall lamentable night' and they glimpsed a 'maruellous huge mountain of yce, which surpassed all the rest that euer we sawe.'

July 4, 1836
The irascible political rebel, William Lyon Mackenzie, started his new paper **The Constitution** to mark the 60th anniversary of the American Declaration of Independence.

July 7, 1620
Champlain arrived at Tadousac with his wife Hélène, who did not remain in New France. She enchanted the Indian girls and children, who followed her about, fingering her fine ribbons, when they could, and begging her to sing.

A View of Quebec from the Heights of the opposite Side of the River, by James Peachey.
The Public Archives of Canada

'From the Island of Orleans to Quebec is one league, and I arrived there on July the third. On arrival I looked for a place suitable for our settlement, but I could not find any . . . better situated than the point of Quebec, so called by the natives, which was covered with nut-trees. . . . The first thing we made was our storehouse, to put our supplies under cover, and it was promptly finished by the diligence of everyone and the care I took in the matter. . . . I continued the construction of . . . three main buildings of two stories . . . three fathoms long and two and a half wide. . . . Distant six or seven leagues . . . was the place where Jacques Cartier passed the winter. . . . Whilst the . . . workmen were busy . . . I set the rest . . . to make gardens . . . for the purpose of seeing how the whole thing would succeed, particularly since the soil seemed to be very good.'

Samuel de Champlain, 1608.

Joseph Elzéar Bernier was 'Canada's master seaman, who has done everything but bring the North Pole back on deck.' So said C. H Snider, authority on sailing vessels, of the man whose record of July 1, 1909 assured Canada's sovereignty in the Arctic, with these words:

'This memorial is erected today to commemorate the taking possession for the Dominion of Canada of the whole Arctic Archipelago lying to the north of America from longitude 60 degrees west to 141 degrees west up to latitude 90 degrees north. Winter Harbour, Melville Island, Canadian Government Steamer, Arctic, Joseph Elzéar Bernier, Commander.'

In 1869 at the age of 17 this navigator and explorer became master of his father's brigantine. Among the many honours that came to him was the award of the Royal Geographical Society's Back Grant in recognition of the vast knowledge he shared of the twelve expeditions he had made to the Arctic.

OUR GRASS ROOTS

The English history books tell of Ticonderoga, and very briefly; the French talk of the Battle of Carillon, and at very great length, since on July 8, 1758, Montcalm won a great victory over James Abercromby's British forces at Lake Champlain.

Montcalm wrote, 'Without Indians, almost without Canadians or colony troops, alone with Lévis and Bourlamaque and the troops of the line, 3100 fighting men, I have beaten an army of 25,000. . . . What a day for France! What soldiers are ours! Why were they not at Louisbourg?'

This particular terrain seems to have been a natural battleground, for the first encounter between Champlain and the Iroquois took place at the same spot 150 years earlier.

Gentlemen,

The Young Men employed in the Wholesale Warehouses in the City of Hamilton, with due deference to the interests of their employers, desire that a small portion of time should be allowed them for amusement or Rational recreation, and considering that little or no business is done in the wholesale Establishments on Saturdays, are of opinion that the interests of their employers would not be injured by closing their warehouses at 3 o'clock P.M. Saturdays of each week; and that such arrangement would be a source of much enjoyment to them.

(Signed) W. F. Murray, chairman,
Jas. A. Skinner, Secty.
Hamilton, Ont., July 7, 1832.

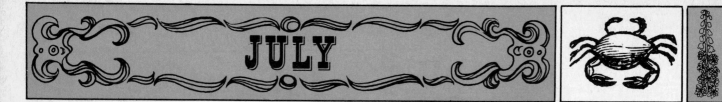

JULY

Tom Thompson.

The Public Archives of Canada.

Mrs. Charnok . . . informs the ladies . . . that she cleans and makes to look equal to new Ostrich, Down, and White Satin Feathers.

Advt., Quebec 'Telegraph', July 13, 1816.

'I believe that one of the chief ingredients in human happiness is a capacity for enjoying the blessings we possess'.

Catherine Parr Traill, who came to Upper Canada in 1832.

OUR GRASS ROOTS

'To the memory of Tom Thomson, Artist, Woodsman and Guide, who was drowned in Canoe Lake, July 8, 1917. He lived humbly but passionately with the wild. It made him brother to all untamed things in nature. It drew him apart and revealed itself wonderfully to him. It sent him out from the woods only to show these revelations through his art; and it took him to itself at last.'

This inscription is on the tablet to the memory of Tom Thomson, who died at 40, as the result of a canoe accident in Algonquin Park. Thoreau MacDonald, himself a painter, and the son of J. E. H. MacDonald, of the famous **Group of Seven**, said of Thomson, 'The north woods were in his bones and he brought sketches out of the bush as naturally as a hunter brings out fish or partridges.'

If you have an idea that the Far North is peaceful and quiet read what explorer-author Ernest Thompson Seton wrote in 'The Arctic Prairies' on July 16, 1907 about Fort Resolution, where there were hundreds of dogs in the smallest villages, all yelping and fighting throughout the night as well as the day. 'It is the worst dog-cursed spot I ever saw; not a square yard but is polluted by them; no article can be left on the ground but will be carried off, torn up, defiled . . . In a short walk, about 200 yards, I passed 86 dogs.'

In the first part of the 18th century, the barter scale between the Hudson's Bay Company and the Indians was:
  1 beaver skin for 1½ lbs. crude tobacco
  1 beaver skin for 2 combs
  1 beaver skin for 2 small hatchets
  6 beaver skins for 1 blanket
12 beaver skins for 1 gun.

The Hudson's Bay Company drew an estimated $100,000,000 out of the fur trade to 1857.

JULY

St. John's Fire 1892. *The Public Archives of Canada.*

DID YOU KNOW THAT

When Sergeant Major James Thompson came to Quebec with General Wolfe's army in 1793, he built a house which remained in the possession of his descendants until 1957.

The Thompson place, now known as Eskimo House, was purchased by the Quebec Commission on Historic Monuments. In addition to serving as a meeting place, a library and museum will be developed. At the opening function on July 13, 1965, a buffet offered curried whale meat, seal in Spanish sauce, Arctic char, whale skin paté, and whale salad. The curry was an adaptation for the Quebec palate.

Life for the little ones in the early days of the Red River pioneers was quite unlike what we know today. Since there was no milk, they were fed fish broth during the first year — and throve on it. An orange had to be described for they had never seen one. We are told that a man paid twenty-five cents (a large sum in that day) for an apple so that his children might see what it was like. They kept it on the piano, and did not think it strange that they had the piano long before the apple. They used a buffalo robe as a toboggan to slide down the river bank. The great treat of the week came after the baking of bread in the large outside oven. The children mixed flour and molasses which they browned and ate as candy.

The Anglican clergyman of Upper Canada, Featherstone Lake Osler and his wife, Ellen Free Pickton, had not one famous son but four. The whole world knew the youngest, Sir William Osler, The Father of Clinical Medicine, who was born July 12, 1849. But of the family of six boys and three girls, three more won distinction: Featherston Osler, the judge; Britton Bath Osler, the lawyer; and Sir Edmund Boyd Osler, the banker.

Each year, Trinity Church, Bond Head, Ont., holds a special service for doctors, physicians and surgeons, to honour Sir William Osler and his father, who was the first rector in 1842.

In the 1800's, the farmers' wives served a most delicious pumpkin loaf, made of boiled pumpkin and cornmeal, which was baked in long loaves and eaten hot from the oven with slathers of freshly churned butter.

Decorative carvings such as one finds on a ship or gabled house date back a long time in our legends. Icelandic history records a carving of a maple tree made about 1014, in Vinland. Was that Cape Cod? Or Labrador? No one is sure. The Icelanders called these artistic creations 'Husasnotra' or 'House-neat.'

To remove a splinter, apply a hot poultice of strong yellow soap and brown sugar.

The place name Toronto occurs for the first time on any document in a manuscript map dated 1673, now preserved in a library of Paris, France.

The furtraders situated at Fort Chipewyan accumulated a great many books to while away the winter months, so that the post was referred to as the 'Athens of the North.'

Bear Fat Pastry
1½ cups flour
½ tsp. salt
⅓ cup bear fat (from a little black bear that was eating berries).
Makes rich white pastry.

JULY

OUR GRASS ROOTS

The 'Macleod Gazette', July 17, 1896 wrote:

Jerry Potts is dead. Through the whole of the North West, in many parts of Eastern Canada and in England, this announcement will excite sorrow. Jerry Potts was a type fast disappearing.... A half breed, he had the distinction of being a very potent factor in the discovery and settlement of the western part of the North West Territories. When Colonels French and Macleod left their wearied and almost helpless columns at Sweet Grass in '74, after a march of 900 miles and a vain search for 'Whoop-Up', it was the veriest accident that they found Jerry Potts, who as a modern Moses was to lead them out of the desert and bring them to the end of their difficulties. He took Macleod's column straight as a die to Whoop-Up.

For years he stood between the police on one side and his natural friends the Indians on the other and his influence always made for peace.

Jerry Potts is dead but his name lives and will live. 'Faithful and true' is the character he leaves behind him — the best monument of a valuable life.

Jerry Potts at Fort MacLeod, 1874. The Public Archives of Canada

The ruby, signifying freedom, charity, dignity and divine power, is the precious regal birthstone for July.

Heard in Saskatchewan, during the dirty thirties – 'It'll get better. God didn't give us all this fertile land for nothing. You'll see.'

Boil three or four onions in a pint of water. Then with a gilding brush do over all your glasses and frames and rest assured that flies will not light on the articles which have been washed. This may be used without apprehension, as it will not do the least injury to the frames.

'1865 Almanac and Register', New Brunswick.

OLD TIMOTHY

'When an ole-time cowboy sez 'bout a feller, 'Ye kin ride the river with him', ye know he's O.K.'

Blueberries for Winter (Indian recipe)

Boil berries down till thick. Spread berry paste on big leaves to dry. Stack up, with little sticks, like legs, between to let the wind through. Store under roof of cabin in dry place.

DATES OF INTEREST

July 1784
Sir John Johnson reported that Loyalists who had left the early colonies to settle in Upper Canada numbered 1,568 men, 626 women, 1,492 children and 90 servants.

July 1854
Six Nations Indians offer to fight the Queen's enemies anywhere.

July 17, 1648
A temperance meeting was held at Sillery, Quebec, the first in America.

July 18, 1867
Jefferson Davis, President of the Confederate States through the Civil War, attended 'The Rivals' at Theatre Royal, Coté St., Montreal.

July 18, 1818
The first shower of grasshoppers fell on the Red River District, hiding the sun and devouring every green thing.

July 18, 1900
Postal authorities complained that skunk pelts were sent in sacks through the mail, forcing the clerks to air all the letters.

Alexander Mackenzie, fur-trader and explorer, came to the end of the first crossing of the North American continent on July 20, 1793. His Journal of the voyage to the Pacific Coast tells of the days of arrival.

'July 20, 1793. We rose at a very early hour this morning, when I proposed to the Indians to run down our canoe, or procure another at this place.... They turned a deaf ear, as they imagined that I should be satisfied with having come in sight of the sea .... Our stock was reduced to 20 lbs. of pemmican; 15 lbs. of rice and 6 lbs. of flour among 10 half-starved men, in a leaky vessel and on a barbarous coast.

'July 21. We coasted along the land at about West-South-West for six miles ..... We landed and took possession of a rock ... which admitted of our defending ourselves with advantage, in case we should be attacked.... I directed the people to keep watch by two in turn, and laid myself down in my cloak.

'July 22. Two canoes now approached the shore, and ... five men with their families landed very quietly. These Indians were of a different tribe from those which we had already seen, as our guide did not understand their language. I now mixed up some vermilion in melted grease and inscribed, in large characters, on the South-East face of the rock on which we had slept last night, this brief memorial – 'Alexander Mackenzie, from Canada, by land, the twenty second of July, one thousand seven hundred and ninety-three.'

Visitors are welcome to the Parliament Buildings, Ottawa, any day except Christmas and New Year's Day, from 9 a.m. until 5.30 p.m. Constables of the Parliamentary Staff act as guides and really seem proud to explain the interesting rooms, especially to youngsters.

JULY

DID YOU KNOW THAT

During the days of the Cariboo Gold Rush in 1862, the miners on the trail looked and looked again — and refused to believe their eyes! For there in the jungles of the Harrison were the most unlikely creatures one would expect to see in British Columbia: twenty-one camels.

These camels were the brain-storm of a miner-prospector-freighter, named Frank, who couldn't load enough on his mules. Frank heard that camels could carry 1,000 lbs. for long distances and needed less water. But it didn't turn out too well. First, the camels had soft feet that were used to sand, and the rocks of the Cariboo wore them out. Second, the miners complained about the stench of the beasts, but endured it. Not so the horses and mules, who were literally driven wild by the odour. They bolted off the road on the trail to Quesnel. They plunged into rivers. They did anything to get away from the camel smell.

When other packers sued him for damages, Frank knew he was beaten, and turned the camels loose on the Thomson Flats and Cache Creek, where they were last seen at the turn of the century.

ઈલ ઈલ

Camels in British Columbia. Department of Recreation and Conservation   Victoria B.S.

In real movie style, a lone desperado on a high bluff pointed his double-barrelled shotgun and held up the Qu'Appelle — Prince Albert mail stage on July 17, 1886, the first such robber in what is now Saskatchewan.

He was caught some time after a clean getaway and established as one Garnett of 'Blameless reputation.' Although he reiterated his innocence, conclusive evidence piled up which netted him fourteen years' imprisonment.

In the early days of settlement, when property could not be defended, such severe sentences punished crimes involving robbery and shooting.

Summer Fashions from Godey's Lady's Book.

Mitts are ugly except on a beautiful hand.
As a rule, hats for the seaside are eccentric and fantastical in the extreme.
For tennis, some charming gowns are made of cream woollen material, with jerseys to match, embroidered in gay colours.
Apple red is the name of a new shade in veiling. Soft and pretty, it throws a becoming bloom on the complexion.

The News and Ottawa Valley Advocate, July, 1885.

Yukon Railway Pass – 1899.

Not transferable, must be signed in ink or blood. The undersigned assumes all risks of damage to person and baggage ... must be ready to 'mush' behind at the crack of the driver's whip .... Passengers falling into the mud must first find themselves and then remove soil from garments as the Red Line Transportation Company does not own the country. Remarks forbidden if the horse climbs a tree. Each must retain seat if the sled drops through the ice, until bottom of the lake is reached, when all are expected to walk ashore.... If the passenger has but one lung, he may inhale the fresh air to capacity of said lung, but no more will be allowed. I accept the above conditions. Signature ——

Notices of deaths, unless accompanied by a special fee, will be restricted to two lines and a half, but an enclosed five-dollar bill (silver taken at a discount) will ensure a double-headed double black-edged column, devoted to praises of the deceased, and enumerating his particular vices (if he had any) ... For a gratuity, however, of twenty dollars, the editor guarantees to indite a delightfully sublime and pathetic obituary in blank verse, to put in a personal appearance, if requested at the wake, and ere morning dawns amidst the ruins of broken heads and broken bottles, so customary at these mournful family gatherings, to pronounce such a eulogy over the dear remains as would bring tears to the eyes of a Dromedary.

'Moodyville Tickler', Burrard Inlet, B.C. July 20, 1878.

ઈલ ઈલ

Regina's first constable was hired in July 1892 for $50 a month and one free uniform. He complained 'It's a trifle uncomfortable when my one suit gets wet'. He looked after licenses for transient traders, billard tables, dogs, and liquor, was in charge of the streets, buildings, public health, market, and general law and order. He rang the town bell at 12, 13, 18 and 19 o'clock every week day. Obtained in 1890, the heavy bell could be heard 15 miles away.

ઈલ ઈલ   *Regina 'Leader', 1905.*

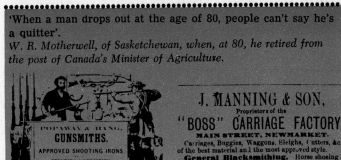

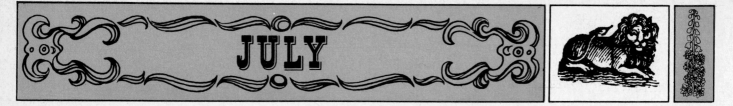

JULY

The Duke of Windsor, while he was Edward, Prince of Wales, bought the Bedingfeld Ranch in Alberta in 1919, and operated it, in absentia, for some years. It was called the EP Ranch (Edward Prince) and the brand mark on the cattle was well known thereabouts.

The Prince wanted to be very informal at his ranch, but as one would expect, the townspeople of nearby High River were both curious and interested. They presented His Royal Highness with a painting by Charles M. Russell, finished in 1915, which depicted the Mounted Police and was called 'When Law Dulls the Edge of Chance'.

OLD TIMOTHY

In the old days a travelling pedlar was on the road to a small village, with an Indian to guide him along the snow-covered paths. It was bitterly cold, yet the almost naked Indian seemed not too uncomfortable. The shivering pedlar said, 'Aren't you cold with so little on?' The Indian asked, 'Your cheeks cold?' When the traveller said 'no', the Indian spoke again, 'Indian all cheek.'

Our first fifty cent pieces were minted in 1870, during the reign of Queen Victoria, when 450,000 coins were distributed. By 1962 there were over four times as many: 1,894,092.

'Heard an Injun rebuke a trader offering an inferior rope cheap, 'In the middle of the rapids, I will not consider the cost of that line'.'

At the Diamond Jubilee, in London, England, in 1897, a large arch bore this legend 'The Granary of the Empire, Free Homes for Millions (in Canada), God Bless the Royal Family.' Again in 1902, at Coronation ceremonies, in the same spot appeared an arch of wheat with the motto, 'Canada, the Granary of the Empire.'

On July 28, 1891, eleven years before the Coronation, the first Harvest Excursion left for the west with 1300 workers, the first of an annual stream of men, young and not-so-young, from all parts of Canada, and England.

Fever for the west had them, but the high wages lured them, too – the highest that had ever been paid transient workers. It started at $1.50 a day but soon it jumped to $2.00; to $3.50 and more. In 1915, the year of the 'bumper crop' that the west is always dreaming about, the pay reached the astronomical $6 to $8 a day.

Huge highly-coloured posters appeared throughout Canada beckoning strong adventurous men. Many a high-school and college boy, many a white-collar man thought to combine a holiday with a chance to see the country and return home with a stake. Some did.

The exact spot where Intendant Jean Talon established the first brewery in Quebec City in 1668 has seen many historical changes. The building above the vault storehouses saw service as a fortress, mansion, Intendant's palace and military headquarters. It was occupied by Richard Montgomery and Benedict Arnold, the American generals who led an invasion of Canada during the Revolutionary War. In a futile siege in 1775, the superstructure of the old building was destroyed but the vaults remained intact, and were re-discovered in 1855.

"Crow Foot at the Pow-wow," by Sidney Hall. The Public Archives of Canada.

DID YOU KNOW THAT

The wise and trustworthy Crowfoot, Chief of the Blackfoot Nation in the 1800's, was often called 'the umbrella chief'. He was inordinately fond of an umbrella which he had received as a present from one of the traders and it was his delight to ride swiftly across the plains holding high this proud possession. Whether it rained or not was of no importance.

Three centuries of life among the Algonquins can be traced through the 2,000 exhibits at the museum of the Abenaki Indians on the Odanak reserve on the St. Francis River, seventy-five miles from Montreal. These include costumes of the tribal chiefs, medicine men, warriors, women and papooses, as well as many examples of early Canadian trapping, hunting and fishing equipment. These Indians excel as carvers, and have many elaborately created drinking scoops, many made with animal designs. An old ritual has it that water must never be drunk directly from the stream, so the scoop is an important possession. As 'sweet-grass basket-makers' the Abenakis are known throughout all of Canada and much of the United States.

Not all the migrant workers took to the gruelling sixteen hour day that started at dawn. The threshing, binding, stooking, hauling, hitching, and sweating wasn't for everybody.

But some liked what they saw on the prairies and stayed on. One was a lad named Gardiner, who was twice to become the Premier of Sasketchewan, and later the Minister of Agriculture in King's cabinet.

Another, John Campbell Bowen, became Lieutenant-Governor of Alberta in 1937.

The Great Eastern, at Heart's Content. 1866. The Public Archives of Canada.

OUR GRASS ROOTS

Samples assayed as 'gold, with a little quartz' started nothing but trouble for Lemon, a grub-staked prospector who made a rich strike in the N.W.T. in 1868. The rush was on, but it brought only hardship, disappointments, madness, fatal accidents and murder. The Stoney Indians reported gold, but because of the many killings, put a taboo on the area, and destroyed the mine markings. The site has never been found, yet the legends of Lemon's Mine are told and re-told whenever oldtimers get together.

A Texas rancher with a somewhat similar name, T. S. Lemons Jr., aged 40, recently found a gold mine that may be worth as much as $200,000,000. This bonanza is supposed to be the lost San Saba mine which the Spaniards abandoned in 1758 when 2,000 Comanche Indians overran their mission.

Samuel de Champlain noted in 1615 that with the Huron and most other Indian tribes the child was considered to be of the clan of the mother, not the father, and that inheritances of possessions and power were through the females.

In Gaspé there is a strange belief that one who pulls three hairs out of his or her head on Sunday morning before church will be happy and contented all week.

'Suppose you do believe too much, it is safer than believing too little.'

'Nature and Human Nature', by Justice Thomas Chandler Haliburton, 1855.

In summertime the sun shines bright
And this is not a trick –
You cannot tell the day from night
'Cause you're in Inuvik.

Pupil, Sir Alexander Mackenzie School, Inuvik, N.W.T.

'With this hand he labors and with the other he protects'.

Motto on the Coat of Arms granted to the colony of Nova Scotia by Charles I in 1625.

'Turn me which way you will, I stand'.

These challenging words were painted on a sign board of an old log cabin about 1880 in the 'black lakes' district, Peterborough, Ontario.

'It is stated that the farmers in the West are trying to adapt the long distance telephone to call the cows home at night.'

The 'Electrical World', July 25, 1896

'Oh, sheep with the crooked horn, where are you? All sheep have milk, but this one gives a gallon'.

This old Gaelic song from Cape Breton Island refers to the tap of the home-made whisky-still.

I was Mephibosheth Stepsure, whose ambition was to be a plain decent farmer. Here, the whole habiliments and expenses of a gentleman were saved; and being a gentleman, I assure you, is a trade which requires costly tools.

'The Letters of Mephibosheth Stepsure', Thomas McCulloch, 1821.

DATES OF INTEREST

July 24, 1883
Captain Matthew Webb was lost while attempting to swim the Whirlpool of the Niagara Rapids. Unlike the many dare-devils who performed stunts at Niagara Falls, he had to his credit a great many successful aquatic displays.

July 27, 1866
The first transatlantic cable was landed at Heart's Content, Nfld. Marconi received the first transatlantic wireless message at St. John's in 1901 and it was from this capital city of Newfoundland that Alcock and Brown set out on the first successful flight across the Atlantic in 1919.

July 29, 1685
Because of the scarcity of regular currency, Jacques de Meulles, intendant of New France, issued 'playing card money'. Although intended as a temporary expedient, it remained in common use until 1759 in French Canada. Cards were used whole, or cut into quarters, halves etc. indicating value. Other unusual money makeshifts included 'phantom' banknotes and 'bons' (meaning 'bon pour' or 'good for').

July 30, 1866
Victoria, B.C. rejoiced at the completion of the Atlantic cable connecting America with dear old England. A meeting at the government buildings, fire-works, bon-fires, and a torch-light procession marked the elation.

AUGUST

OLD TIMOTHY

'Thar wuz so very few wimmin among our earlier settlers that a man would say to a newly arrived lady, very politely, 'Good day, m'am, be ye married?' Ef she answered, 'Yes', he went on his way. Ef she said, 'No', he proposed marriage to her at onct.'

'Islingdingadagurinn'. This is a festival held at Gimli near Winnipeg during the first week of August, in honour of the first Icelandic settlers.

Old tried remedies
Dip a penny in vinegar and rub over fever blisters till they disappear.

Eat a large slice of bread spread with fresh skunk oil morning and evening to cure rheumatism.

Pitch of pine trees will cure sores and boils.

Cayenne pepper and soda will prevent nightmares.

Castor oil will end warts, so they won't come again, if the oil is applied outdoors when the moon is full. As the moon wanes, the warts disappear.

Major G. P. Vanier 22nd. Battalion 1918. The Public Archives of Canada.

OUR GRASS ROOTS

'Je me souviens' ('I remember') is the proud motto of Quebec's Royal 22nd Regiment. Formed in 1914, this first fully-organized French Canadian fighting force is affectionately known as the Van Doos, which is pretty close to the French words 'vingt-deuxième.' Lieutenant George P. Vanier, who was to become General Vanier and the Governor-General of Canada, was with it from the very beginning when it was called the 22nd French-Canadian Battalion.

General Wolfe to his mother:

Louisbourg, August, 1758.

Dear Madam –
Mr. Herbert would have perished of scurvy long since, but he has fallen into good hands and seems to be pretty healthy.

The early season in this country, I mean the months of April and May, are intolerably cold and disagreeable; June and July are foggy; August rainy; September has always a tempest; October is generally a dry fair month; and the winter sets in early in November. Further to the south . . . there is a variety of climate, so that a man may . . . live in perpetual spring or summer. . . . Notwithstanding disadvantages, and . . . the treachery of their neighbours the French, and the cruelty of their neighbours the Indians, worked up to the highest pitch by the former, this will, some time hence be a vast empire, the seat of power and learning.

Nature has refused them nothing, and there will grow a people out of our little spot, England, that will fill this vast space. . . . I am, dear Madam, etc.   J. Wolfe.

August 5, 1793. Many of the natives arrived both from the upper and lower parts of the river, each dressed in a beaver robe. . . . It is an extraordinary circumstance, that these people, who might have taken all the property we left behind us, without the least fear of detection, should leave that untouched, and purloin any of our utensils, which our confidence in their honesty gave them a ready opportunity of taking. Several articles were missing, and as I was very anxious to avoid a quarrel with the natives, in this stage of our journey, I told those who remained near us that their relations had no idea of the mischief that would result from taking our property. I added that the salmon, which was not only their favourite food, but absolutely necessary to their existence, came from the sea which belonged to us white men; and that as we could prevent those fish from coming up, we possessed the power to starve them and their children. They must return all the articles which had been stolen from us. This finesse succeeded.
From Alexander Mackenzie's Journal (arrival at the Pacific coast).

The Queen's Proclamation, uniting Rupert's Land and the North West Territory with Canada; the swearing in of the Hon. A. G. Archibald as Lieutenant-Governor of the new province of Manitoba and also under a separate commission of the N.W.T.; the progress of the expedition all point that another substantial step has been taken towards the Union of British North America. Three years to make this one step, and other steps yet to be taken. The process of Confederation has been slower than its ardent friends anticipated.
'Canadian Illustrated News', Montreal, Aug. 6, 1870.

AUGUST

First party of Doukhobors, near Yorkton. 1899.   *The Public Archives of Canada.*

August 1, 1639
The Jesuits numbered the Hurons at 20,000 persons.

August 1, 1639
The Ursuline Convent was founded with Marie de l'Incarnation as Superior.

August 1690
Montreal was crowded with Hurons, Ottawas, Ojibwas, Pottawatamies, Crees and Nipissings, all come to trade. After a council and warfeast, Frontenac joined the Indians in their antics, partaking of the two oxen and six large dogs that had been minced and cooked with prunes. Two barrels of wine and tobacco added to the enjoyment.

August 3, 1527
Capt. John Rut, of the Royal Navy, sent the first letter from Canada, from St. John's, Nfld. to Henry VIII to give the news from Labrador.

DID YOU KNOW THAT

The early Doukhobors in Saskatchewan were said to harness their women like horses. The truth is that after extreme hardship in 1899, the men went to work on the railroad. The only way the women could plant the soil and produce food was by organizing themselves into groups of twenty and pulling a walking plow.

The mythical 'sea unicorne':
'On the west shoare', the chronicler wrote in Frobisher Bay, August 1571, 'we found a dead fishe floating whiche had in his nose a horn straight and torquet (twisted) of lengthe two yardes lacking two inches.'

   Sir Martin Frobisher's seamen acted in good faith when they presented this rare 'unicorne's horn' to Queen Elizabeth I at Windsor. A similar treasure, but smaller, was sold to Charles I. Did the explorers know that these were the large spiral tusks of the male narwhal? Their ivory fetched large sums in China, where it was used in medicines, and to make vessels that absorbed all poisons.

In spite of the hardships of pioneer life, the women of the Red River area of Manitoba clung to their feminine foibles. A plain mutch covered the head for every day activities, but the frills of the decorative go-to-meeting mutch were carefully treated with an Italian iron heated in the fire. This iron fitted into its own box when not in use, and was loaned as a distinct favour.

   We are told of one woman who in 1860 wrote back home to the old country – 'Dear Elizabeth, Please send me three of the most fashionable bonnet shapes from Mrs. K.'s. There are none to be had up here.'

The gladioli, the birthday flower for August, is the symbol of loyalty, light and innocence, especially the lighter blooms. The darker ones mean doubt, questioning and fears.

'That's what we need. Women who will lead the followers and not follow the leaders'.
Magistrate Emily Murphy (Janey Canuck) in an address to a woman's club.

The Indians call August 'The Green Corn Moon' or 'Opuhoo'wepesim – The Flying Up of Young Duck's Moon'.

The August-born may choose from two birthstones: the peridot (a transparent gem of rich olive green) and the sardonyx, a precious variety of deep warm coloured quartz, the emblem of warmest friendship. Set in gold, the peridot repels night terrors, and brings love.

A Nova Scotian has been discribed as 'hard as nails, soft as butter and as independent as a pig on ice.'

Bear Feet (Thompson Indians)

Place feet in forked stick and singe hair off in fire. Boil in water to loosen skin. Wash his feet good. Boil with salt to eat.

The Roman Emperor Gaius Octavius felt very fortunate in 8 B.C. and took the name Augustus, giving it to the month of August in which he ended the Civil War. At one time it was the sixth, not the eighth month in the calendar, and as such had been known as sextilis.

AUGUST

I have got a character to maintain, and must take care not to lose it, as persons who are perpetually writing very generally do.

'The Letters of Mephibosheth Stepsure' by Thomas McCulloch, 1821.

'Poverty is keen enough without sharpening its edge by pokin' fun at it.'

Justice Thomas Chandler Haliburton, about 1840.

'Wealth will not take care of itself if not vigilantly cared for.'

John Henry Robinson Molson, of the third Canadian generation, who died in 1897.

'A country's wealth is what you walk on.'

Stephen B. Leacock.

⚜ ⚜ ⚜ ⚜ ⚜ ⚜

DATES OF INTEREST

August 9, 1757
Fort William Henry, garrisoned by 2200, capitulated. Indians killed many, whereupon Montcalm cried, 'Kill me, but spare the English who are under my protection.'

August 12, 1856
The Allan Line established, with pioneer ships 'Canadian', 'North American', 'Indian' and 'Anglo Saxon'.

August 13, 1860
Daily Witness, Montreal, first issued.

August 14, 1787
In an investigation into judicial abuses, it is stated that one judge takes wine to excess, before taking his seat on the Bench; and that another habitually disregards the pertinent French law and applies the law of England.

August 15, 1870
Manitoba becomes a province.

August 15, 1893
The Behring Sea Tribunal of Arbitration ruled that Behring Sea be kept open and seals protected.

Susanna Moodie. 1803 ~ 1885.

The Public Archives of Canada.

OUR GRASS ROOTS

Susanna Moodie in 1852 gave us this Indian recipe for broiling fish, suggesting that an epicure would do well to copy it:

Remove entrails but not scales of freshly caught fish. Wash clean, dry with grass, cover with clean hot ashes. When the flesh comes away from the bone, remove ashes, and strip off skin, for a most delectable morsel.

∽ ∽

Louis Philippe Hébert, R.C.A., 1883, C.M.G., 1903, Chevalier of the Legion of Honour in France, who was recognized as the foremost Canadian sculptor of his time, created small statues of the Fathers of Confederation. About two feet tall, they are cherished by private families, clubs and museums. At Fort Beausejour, Aulac, New Brunswick, is one of Sir Charles Tupper, and we are told that a copy is in the Drury Lane Steak House.

At the Chateau de Ramezay, Montreal, one may see those representing Sir John A. Macdonald, Sir Wilfrid Laurier, and Sir George Etienne Cartier.

∽ ∽

Although the beaver has been recognized for very many years as a popular emblem of Canada, it has never been given official status as such by statute or regulation. Through its use on Canadian coins, it has acquired a quasi-official status. The first Canadian postage stamp, issued in 1851, was the 'three-penny beaver' of Sir Sandford Fleming. The beaver appeared also on a medal struck in 1690, popularly known as 'Quebec Liberated'.

⚜ ⚜ ⚜ ⚜ ⚜ ⚜

Among some Indians, it was the custom to shoot a deceased man's pony when he was buried, so that he could ride in the Happy Hunting Grounds.

'England would be better off without Canada; it keeps her in a prepared state for war at a great expense and constant irritation'.

Napoleon I, in 'Diary of P. Malcolm at St. Helena', 1817.

⚜ ⚜ ⚜ ⚜ ⚜ ⚜

For over a hundred years the lumberjacks in the Ottawa Valley were singing —

'We're the jolliest bunch of fellows,
That ever you could find,
The way we spend our winter months,
Is hurling down the pine.
You can hear those axes ringing,
Until the sun goes down.'

For over a hundred years the axes that they use have been made at Aylmer, Quebec, by a firm that was founded in 1855 by Henry Walters, a cutlery maker from Sheffield, England. The Walters company is the largest in the Commonwealth, with an output each year of 250,000 axes.

'The telephone is exciting some interest and I have no doubt will become popular in Canada.'

Rev. Thomas Henderson made this statement on August 14, 1877 when he received the first shipment of telephones for Canada, eight wooden hand and eight wooden box telephones. He had persuaded the Bells to come to Canada from Scotland in 1870 and was Alexander Graham Bell's special Canadian agent.

Rev. James Nisbet.
The Public Archives of Canada.

DATES OF INTEREST

August 1866
Rev. James Nisbet and party of ten settled on the North Saskatchewan River, naming the place Prince Albert.

August 1649
Laurent Berman became the first practising notary in Canada.

August 15, 1866
College of Ottawa, by Royal Charter, became University of Ottawa. A century later, Mme. George P. Vanier, wife of the Governor-General, was installed as chancellor – the first lay chancellor and the second woman to become titular head of a Canadian University. The first woman chancellor was Mrs. Frank M. Ross of the U. of British Columbia.

August 1687
A mission Indian told Denonville – 'He who oversets a wasp's nest, must kill them, lest they sting him'. Denonville had overset the Senecas, but had not hurt them. They were preparing for revenge.

DID YOU KNOW THAT

The 150th anniversary of the founding of the Province of New Brunswick by King George III in 1784 was commemorated with the issuance of a special 2-cent stamp on August 16, 1934. This coincided with other sesquincentennial anniversary celebrations. The brown 2-cent stamp showed the Great Seal of the Province which was forwarded in 1785 to Thomas Carleton, Governor of the Colony from the Court of St. James, but which is now thought to be lost.

The design is of 'a ship sailing up a river, on the borders of which is a new settlement with lofty pines on each side, destined to naval purposes.' The motto 'Spem Reduxit', 'It brings back hope', relates to the circumstances involved in the establishment of the colony.

August 10 is the Festival of St. Lawrence. Since Jacques Cartier found shelter in a pleasant bay on that anniversary in 1534, he gave the name to the mighty St. Lawrence. What do we know of this saint whose name is ever with Canadians? Born between 210-220, either in Spain or Italy, this evangelist died, not ordained, in 258. He was martyred by fire during the time of Emperor Valerian. A painting of him by Fra Angelico is in the Vatican, by Le Sueur in the Louvre, by Titian in Venice and several are in Madrid and other parts of Spain.

The wonders of Canada include the remarkable Reversing Falls of Saint John, New Brunswick, which are caused by the tides of the Bay of Fundy. In a rocky gorge in the old part of town, this phenomenon results from the alternate flooding and pulling on the lower Saint John River.

OLD TIMOTHY

'Old-timers were kinda strict about one thing. The only folks they asked to join them at meals were strangers or friends.'

Expressive Newfoundland sayings:

As fine a man as ever hove a gallus (suspender) over his shoulder.

As good as water ever wet.

As straight as a gun barrel.

AUGUST

Canadian Red Cross Society

A quickly stitched insignia of red and white factory cotton was the first Red Cross Flag in Canada. Serving with a volunteer ambulance brigade during the Northwest Rebellion of 1885, Surgeon-Major (later Major-General) George Sterling Ryerson felt the need of a distinguishing mark to direct the wounded to his horse-drawn wagon-hospital. The emblem he created is in the John Ross Robertson Collection of the Toronto Public Library.

General Ryerson was named chairman in 1896 when the Canadian branch of the British National Society for Aid to the Sick and Wounded, subtitled the Red Cross, was formed. In 1909 a special act of the Canadian Parliament established the Canadian Red Cross Society as a corporate body. Each province has a division and in all there are more than 1000 branches.

'To him I owe my fondness for reading, my familiarity with the Bible . . . The remembrance of his high principles, his cheerfulness, and truly Christian character is never absent from my mind.' *Joseph Howe, on the death of his father, 1835.*

OUR GRASS ROOTS

Blazing a small spruce, he wrote — 'To whom it may concern. I do, this day, locate and claim by right of discovery, 500 feet, running upstream from this notice. Located this 17th day of August, 1896. G. W. Carmack.'

'Discovery Day', the territorial holiday which the Yukon celebrates annually on August 17, marks this strike by George W. Carmack and his Indian companions, Skookum Jim and Tagish Charlie. It was the start of the Klondike Gold Rush which brought thousands along the 'Trail of '98' and resulted in the Yukon Territory becoming separate from the North West Territories in 1898.

The three who found gold went on information from Robert Henderson, the first to be convinced that the Yukon was rich. Following the rules of the 'Yukon Order of Pioneers', he broadcast his news, but **never staked a claim himself.** In the mad frenzy of new millionaires, no one thought to find Henderson with news of the discovery, until the whole creek had been staked.

Explorer Martin Frobisher was unhappily involved in Canada's first and least successful gold rush to Kodlunarn (White Man's) Island on Frobisher Bay in the Arctic about 1577. Old Eskimo tales tell of a dozen ships at anchor while busy crews dug for the precious metal. Adventurous Frobisher, seeking the Northwest Passage to 'the ritch Countrey of Cataya (Cathay)', and excited by the bonus of what he thought to be gold on the island, lost out on both counts.

DATES OF INTEREST

August 18, 1843
George Brown and his father began **The Banner**, a free church paper in Toronto. He later became editor of the Toronto **Globe**.

August 21, 1775
Generals Schuyler and Montgomery, with 1,000 Americans, come to Canada to invite the inhabitants to rebel.

August 23, 1541
Cartier reached Stadacona.

August 23, 1834
The Whig, Kingston, U.C., first appeared.

August 23, 1835
Red River settlers complain against the monopoly and oppression of the Hudson's Bay Company

August 1762
Capt. Peabody and his family left Massachussets to become the first permanent English residents of New Brunswick, where Saint John, N.B. now stands.

Forget dull days; ignore showers;
Count the shining hours.

OLD TIMOTHY

'In the Yukon folks sed 'We hev so many uncommon men hereabouts, they become common, jest as in Heaven, angels air nobodies!'

'It's better to trade bulls than bullets.'
Cyrus Stephen Eaton, Nova Scotia-born financier, after he had sent bulls to the Soviet Union.

SOURDOUGH ANTIQUE SHOP
Oposite the old river boats
Whitehorse, Yukon Territory.

For their dances and gatherings, Eskimos use their only musical invention, the ayayut, a drum-like instrument.

Dr. Frederick Banting was only thirty-two years old and just one year out of Medical School, when in 1923 he was awarded the Nobel Prize for a great discovery in medicine that was to be a blessed help to sufferers of diabetes. He brought his idea to Professor J. J. R. Macleod, head of the department of physiology in the University of Toronto, and with the help of several fellow-workers demonstrated the usefulness of insulin. The Caroline Institute in Stockholm offered the Nobel Award to 'Macleod and Banting'. Dr. Macleod divided his share with Dr. J. B. Collip; and Dr. Banting with Dr. Charles Herbert Best. However Dr. Banting always pointed out that he ascride equal share in the discovery to Dr. Best, a
biochemist, who was then twenty-four years old.

'We have upwards of one hundred licensed houses and perhaps as many more which retail spirituous liquors without license; so that the business of one half of the town is to sell rum and the other half to drink it'.
Anonymous resident of Halifax, N.S., 1760.

Sir Frederick Banting, circa 1938-1939
The Public Archives of Canada

'The Molson family has maintained and preserved its position and influence by steady, patient industry, and every member should be a real worker and not rely on what it has been.'

John Henry Robinson Molson, of the third Canadian generation, who died in 1897.

'The minute man put foot on Canadian soil, discharged a gun and shot a bird, he interferred with Nature; thus, it is up to man to balance Nature.'
Jack Miner, O.B.E.

DID YOU KNOW THAT

A shoemaker in Charlottetown, P.E.I., ran a 'do-it-yourself-mint' by issuing leather notes, valued at two shillings, sixpence. It happened in 1836 when the perfectly solvent island was suffering a shortage of actual coins. The cobbler acted with the authorization of the P.E.I. Legislature and the treasury redeemed the leather money soon after.

'Uphold the right .'
The motto of the Royal Canadian Mounted Police is not 'Get your man' but 'Maintiens le droit' (Uphold the right), which indeed the force has done since August 1873 when 300 were enrolled for Fort Garry, under Commander George Arthur French.

At the outset, Prime Minister John A. Macdonald changed the name from North West Mounted Rifles, to Police, and made the crimson tunic official.

In 1904, King Edward VII honoured the force with the prefix 'Royal'. Later another change made it the Royal Canadian Mounted Police (RCMP) with headquarters in Ottawa.

Unhappy about heavy drinking, in the late 1800's, some Ontario citizens planned a Temperance Colony in Sasketchewan. The vanguard of thirty-five founded the City of Saskatoon on August 20, 1882, complete with pole raising by the leader, John N. Lake. Immigration brought growth and prosperity, with city status by 1906.

Indians called the succulent saskatoon berry, which covered the area, 'A carpet of flowers-mis-sask-quah-too-min'. The musical name appealed to Lake, and Saskatoon it has been called ever since.

The early French Canadian settlers made wonderful bread in their outdoor bake-ovens of stone and clay. Especially good was an extra large loaf weighing fully 6 pounds, which was called 'Mocassin Bread'. On the golden crust could be seen the cross, which the head of the family had traced on the unbaked dough with a knife point — his way of saying "Thanks to God for the good bread.'

Indian legends and place names have come to us through French and English settlers with interesting and amusing results. These verses are from the well-known poem of the voluminous writer Prof. James De Mille, who was born in New Brunswick on August 23, 1836.

'Sweet maiden of Passamaquoddy,
Shall we seek for communion of souls
Where the deep Mississippi meanders
Or the distant Saskatchewan rolls.

Ah no! in New Brunswick we'll find it —
A sweetly sequestered nook —
Where the sweet gliding Skoodawaskooksis
Unites with the Skoodawabskook.'

AT GULL LAKE, AUGUST, 1810
Quiet were all the leaves of the poplars,
Breathless the air under their shadow,
As Keejigo spoke of these things to her heart
In the beautiful speech of the Saulteaux.

The flower lives on the prairie,
The wind in the sky,
I am here my beloved;
The wind and the flower.

The crane hides in the sand-hills,
Where does the wolverine hide?
I am here my beloved,
Heart's blood on the feathers
The foot caught in the trap.

Take the flower in your hand,
The wind in your nostrils:
I am here my beloved;
Release the captive,
Heal the wound under the feathers.

Duncan Campbell Scott, 1862-1947.

THE ILLUSTRATED LONDON NEWS

THE PRINCE OF WALES AT MONTREAL.

THE CRYSTAL PALACE, OPENED BY HIS ROYAL HIGHNESS AUGUST 25.

THE PRINCE OPENING THE INDUSTRIAL EXHIBITION IN THE CRYSTAL PALACE.

DID YOU KNOW THAT

Edward Albert, Prince of Wales, who later reigned as Edward VII, rushed from one important ceremony to another on August 25, 1860. Honouring the most impressive and glittering of Montreal's trade expositions, His Royal Highness opened the Crystal Palace at St. Catharine and University Streets, a reproduction of the original structure for the Great Exposition in London, England'nine years earlier. The Palace continued to attract many, even when it was moved, after several years, to Fletcher's Field.

The colourful inaugural ceremony over, the Prince and his retinue were whisked off to preside at the dedication of the new Victoria Bridge. Local dignitaries, press representatives and the general public dashed like mad from the Palace to the Bridge. All in all, it was quite a day for Montrealers.

∽ ∽

When the Acadian French held their first convention at Memramcook, N.B. in July 1881, they decided to choose as their National Feast Day L'Assomption (August 15th) instead of St. Jean Baptiste's Day (June 24th) adopted by the Canadian French.

∽ ∽

'The Gibraltar of Canada' is what Louisbourg, on Cape Breton Island, turned out to be. Started in 1717, it took 25 years to build, with Louis XV, of France, complaining every step of the way that it was costing him too much. This bastion was, as those who are restoring it find, a very complete settlement with several churches, taverns, meeting-places, a hospital, a theatre and a large ballroom.

It held out for 48 days when the British besieged it, thus giving some extra time to those guarding Quebec. After the capture of Quebec, the British returned to Louisbourg and executed military manoeuvres that reduced the huge stone citadel to ruins.

'Oil Fever'
When oil was struck at Turner Valley near Calgary, just before the war in 1914, fever raged, some say madness. The beautiful C.P.R. Palliser Hotel was thronged with speculators. The 'Calgary Herald' listed these regulations for armchair well drillers:

1. No well shall be drilled before 6 A.M. or after 3 P.M., as operations are liable to disturb the paying guests' . . . beautiful dreams of vast wealth and permanent gushers.
2. No more than one well shall be drilled in each leather chair. . . . It is exhausting to the furniture.
3. No well shall be drilled in a tone of voice which is audible within the three mile zone, and causes the sky-light to flutter.
4. No well shall be drilled nearer than one foot from any door, window or passage-way, and no disputes shall be indulged in, or any lease located in such areas.
5. No dry holes will be tolerated in the lobby. All wells brought in must be in the thousand barrel class, or larger.
6. All shares offered are of the gilt-edge variety. No need to call for the prospectus of the company. Just throw your money up and get your receipt. You can later pass it on to your friends for a better consideration.
7. No well drilled in the lobby shall stop at shallow sand. Every well must run down to deep pay and represent an outlay of not less than $100,000.

At Niagara, before the Hon. Judge Alcock, the trial of George Nemiers and Mary London, alias Mary Osborn, for murder of the late Mr. Bartholomew London, of Saltfleet, by poison. The Attorney General in a pathetic address to the Jury called attention to duty. The Jury delivered them guilty. The Judge, who had judged with mercy, now with mildness passed the dreadful sentence — to be executed. A numerous concourse of people attended the execution.
'Upper Canada Gazette,' or 'American Oracle', York, August, 1801.

Le Révérend Père Paul Le Jeune de la Compagnie de Jésus.
The Public Archives of Canada.

In spite of a record of embezzlement, 45 year old François Bigot was appointed the last intendant of New France. He arrived in Quebec, August 26, 1748. Fraudulent conduct brought him great personal wealth, but news of his profligacy shocked even the court circles of France, and he was brought to trial at the Châtelet, Paris. Although his defence filled 1200 pages, he was fined, made to restore 1,500,000 livres, imprisoned in the Bastille and banished forever. The nobility vied to possess the priceless objet d'arts he had plundered.

History tells us that Canadian Madame Angélique des Meloizes Péan, Bigot's 'little Pompadour', was overcome by remorse and spent her last days in charitable works.

Whether they were built in Quebec, Nova Scotia or New Brunswick, there was romance in the names of the early Canadian ships, such as 'Banker's Daughter', 'Go-ask-her', 'Flying Cloud', 'Sovereign of the Seas', 'Lightning', 'Spray', 'White Wings', 'Glooscap', 'Toboggan', 'Ocean Nymphe', 'Tea Taster', 'Caribou', and the 'Queen of Beauty'.

OUR GRASS ROOTS

Oldtimers used to tell of the days when Pat Burns drove 3000 head of cattle through Eighth Ave., Calgary. In 1890, this 'Cattle King' established the firm of P. Burns and Co., Limited which became one of the biggest businesses of its kind in the world with branches in London and Yokohama.

He started with nothing except a willingness to take on any job, no matter how difficult. When the railroads, mining outfits and lumber camps needed beef, Pat was ready to supply them. The saga of how he got beef to the Yukon in the 1898 Gold Rush is typical of the man. No one thought he could get his cattle to Dawson City, a good 1000 miles further than any have ever been sent. First Pat sent his herds from Vancouver by boats as far as he could. Then they were driven through wild mountain passes. On the brinks of the Lewes River, the cattle were slaughtered, and the beef sent down stream to Dawson City, where men hungry for steaks were more than ready to pay good prices. After that initiation, supplying the Yukon and Alaska was easy for Pat.

Like everything else about Pat's personality, the cake at his 75th birthday party was big — two tons big. 15,000 pieces were given to friends, for he seemed to have just about that many. Although he was filled with pride at the birthday present from Prime Minister R. B. Bennett, appointing him a Senator, he reminded those about him, 'I'm a rancher.'

～⊙～ ～⊙～

Horace Greeley served during the Territorial days in the 1900's as a member of the Legislature, with a constituency from Swift Current to Medicine Hat, from the International Boundary to the Saskatchewan River. He was as interesting as his famous journalist uncle of the same name, who so vehemently advised 'Go West, young men, go West, and grow up with the country.' The younger Horace was a colourful part of early pioneer and then ranch life. He left instructions that a field boulder was to be taken from his ranch, placed on his grave, and marked 'I'm off to the last round-up'.

OLD TIMOTHY

'In the west, folks usta say thar wuz hundreds of funerals, afore anyone died nacherally.'

The inner bark of the sumach, roasted and made into a powder, was used as a remedy for the ague in 1830. A teaspoonful was administered between the hot and cold fits with beneficial results.

～⊙～ ～⊙～

'The beaver does not improve, and becomes extinct rather than change.'
Sir John William Dawson, naturalist, 1863.

DATES OF INTEREST

August 24, 1820
A pig entered the Bank of Montreal, St. James St., probably unaware of the law that the Town Crier should proclaim the news of a lost pig. Similar announcements were made at church.

August 27, 1793
Toronto, capital of the newly created province of U.C., called York, to honour Duke of York, by John Graves Simcoe, the first Lieut. Governor. The garrison fired the first royal salute.

August 27, 1841
Upper Canada Academy, by royal charter, became Victoria College, endowed with university powers.

August 28, 1632
Father Le Jeune sent the provincial of his order the first letter of 'Relations of the Jesuits'. (The fort at Quebec, some huts on the Island of Montreal, at Three Rivers and at Tadousac and a few fishermen's log cabins on the St. Lawrence were about all there was then to show for the discoveries, toil and suffering of Verrazano, Cartier, Roberval, Champlain, La Roche and De Monts.)

SEPTEMBER

Port Alfred.

The Public Archives of Canada

'Kingdom of the Saguenay'

It was really Jacques Cartier, discoverer of Canada, who so named the rich and beautiful domain which he approached on his 1535-36 voyage. His narratives read – 'We got under way . . . on the first day of September, to go towards Canada, and . . . there are three islands in the middle of the said large river, across which is a river, very deep and fast, which is the river and road of the kingdom and land of the Saguenay.'

In this thriving Quebec area where the Montagnais Indians once roamed, we have Chicoutimi, Arvida, Port Alfred, Kenogami and Bagotville.

Everybody knows the love story of Lord Horatio Nelson and the beautiful Lady Hamilton. But history has not given us the name of the Quebec beauty that England's great naval hero loved so wildly when he was 22.

At the time, Nelson was on the 'Albermarle' in the West Indies trade, which stopped at Quebec City in the autumn of 1780. There he became so attached to a French Canadian girl that he determined to leave his ship and marry her. Only strong action on the part of a fellow ship-member saved him from what was then considered certain ruin.

• •

As with our postage stamps, there is much for the discerning to note in our coins. In addition to the effigies of sovereigns, coronets, armorial ensigns, maple wreaths, coins at various times have depicted our history with designs such as canoes, manned by Indians and voyageurs, the Northern Lights, fishing schooners, antlered caribou heads, Parliament Buildings, John Cabot's ship 'The Matthew,' beavers and maple leaves.

OUR GRASS ROOTS

Country school teachers were always leaving to get married. The school trustees complained bitterly that they seemed to be running a free matrimonial bureau. In her book 'With the West in her Eyes', Kathleen Strange tells that they made the new teacher promise not to marry for six months. Nor did she, until the day after the term expired.

Get your bear — that's easy, if you go where bears are, and shoot straight. Then skin your bear. If the flies in the bush are bad, that will be a long two hours. After that, there's two weeks of scraping fat. Still want that bearskin hat?

The erection of a church or chapel generally precedes that of a school-house in Upper Canada, but the mill and tavern invariably precede both.

Winter Studies and Summer Rambles by Anna Jameson, 1837.

What sort of prizes do you suppose attracted competitors at the fairs out west in the 1880's? Cash awards were most popular, of course. In the categories of Red Fife wheat, oxen, saddle horses, lady riders, Berkshire boars and Durham bulls, the winners were delighted with their booty of an $18 suit, a set of ox harness, a pair of $8 riding breeches, a $7.50 clothes wringer, 1000 roof shingles and a $6 rocking chair.

Marking Saskatchewan's entry into Confederation on Sept. 1, 1905, there were many festivities. The **Regina Leader** describes 'Pushball' on Inaugural Day, Sept. 4, as 'an impossible pastime. At the conclusion of the Royal Northwest Mounted Police musical ride, six riders removed their tunics, and took part, three to a side. The ball, an immense inflated sphere of leather, from England, was propelled by the horses' knees. One of the horses struck the ball with its shoe . . . causing it to collapse, and the game to finish prematurely.'

Canadians find many a language puzzler travelling from coast to coast, for words and expressions have a way of changing their meanings. Newfoundland has a particularly strange word lore – strange that is to the visitor. The Newfoundlanders do just fine. 'Walking about' means to be unemployed; a 'beaver' is a dram at eleven in the morning, sometimes called a 'levener': 'doolamaun' is dulse or kelp; a 'tickle' is a narrow strait; a 'growler' is an iceberg; a 'banker' is a fisherman off the Grand Banks; 'Methodist bread' is raisin bread; and a 'scoff' is a quickly served meal on a boat, generally of pork, cabbage and potatoes. And even if you learn that a Dolly Varden is a large mug for tea, how will that help you on the West Coast, where a Dolly Varden is a special variety of trout?

Colbert in a diatribe to Intendant Jean Baptiste Talon in 1668, said succinctly, 'In countries where everybody labors, and in Canada in particular, there is food for all, and abundance can never come to them except through abundance of men.... It would be well to double the taxes and duties of bachelors who do not marry at 18 ... and as to those who seem to have utterly foresworn marriage, it would be expedient to increase their taxes, to deprive them of all honours, and even to attach to them some mark of infamy ...'

Alberta:
In token of the love which thou hast shown
For this wide land of freedom, I have named
A province vast, and for its beauty famed
By thy dear name to be hereafter known.

Marquis of Lorne, Governor General of Canada, 1878-1883, penned these lines to his wife, Princess Louise Caroline Alberta, after a visit to the West, when they named the province. Alberta entered Confederation on Sept. 1, 1905.

DID YOU KNOW THAT

In September 1903, when railway construction worker Fred Larose away up beyond North Bay, Ontario, threw his blacksmith hammer at what he thought were the gleaming eyes of a fox, he hit the richest silver vein in the world. Because cobalt showed in the ore, the place was named Cobalt. The first 'SILVER KINGS OF THE NORTH', Timmins, the McMartin brothers and Dave Dunlap, paid Larose $30,000 for his claim.

In 1644 a labourer in French Canada was paid 30 cents a day, with board.
   By 1796, he was receiving 60 cents a day in summer, but only 55 cents in winter (shorter hours?).
   In 1852 in Nova Scotia, clerical workers received the following wages: boys to 11 years, 19 cents per week
      boys to 14 years, 31 cents per week
      junior clerks, $1.59 per week
      senior clerks (after 15 years), $3.15 per week.
   In 1830 in Montreal, clerks in stores worked for $50 to $100 a year from 6 a.m. to 9 p.m. daily.

• •

For Jamaica — The brig. 'Delight' will certainly sail in eight days, wind and weather permitting.
Nova Scotia Packet and General Advertiser, September, 1786.

DATES OF INTEREST

September 1748
Sulpician Abbé Picquet began a fort at La Présentation (Ogdensburg).

September 1, 1749
Portneuf, with 15 soldiers, built Fort Rouillé which became Toronto.

September 1, 1824
Foundation stone laid of Notre Dame Cathedral, Montreal.

September 2, 1755
Camp Cumberland, Acadia: 'Leit, Jno. Indicut on shore with men to burn a vilige at Petcojak (Petitcodiac?) after they burnt houses and barns they ware about to burn a masshouse a large number of French and Indians ran out of the wood and Fired so they ware obliged to Retreat.'

September 1907
Balloonists exhibited gliding and course-changing at the annual Dominion Exhibition at Sherbrooke, Quebec.

• • • • • • • • • • • • • • • • • • • •

The aster is the September birthday flower and signifies meditation, thoughtfulness and consideration.

OLD TIMOTHY

'When the school board met, one feller sed 'What'll we do with the school house, when all the kids are grown?' "

• •

In days long gone, the Roman year began in March and the seventh month was September, which means seventh in Latin. When Julius Caesar changed the calendar, in 46 B.C., September became the ninth month but kept the same name.

On Sept. 13, 1759, Wolfe's men scaled the cliff to victory on the Plains of Abraham, Quebec City. Both generals, James Wolfe and Louis-Joseph de Montcalm, were mortally wounded.

There may be a victorious general with a finer monument than Wolfe's, but probably none other ever had as many. Visitors to the memorial on the Plains of Abraham will learn from the inscriptions on all four sides that this is actually Wolfe's fifth monument. Unique, too, is the fact that the word 'victorious' was deleted from the original inscription, and that the text is now bilingual.

The first memorial **now** reads 'Here died Wolfe, Sept. 13, 1759'. The last proclaims 'This fifth memorial was erected by the National Battlefields Commission in July 1965 in replacement of the column which was destroyed on March 29, 1963.' This destruction was caused by an alleged separatist.

The Quebec Turf Club, organized in 1789, and the oldest association of its kind in Canada, had its track on the Plains of Abraham, now Battlefield Park, Quebec City.

Aurora, York County, Ontario, was given the name of the mythological goddess of dawn, because it is most fair in the early morning. There is also a township Dawn, dating from 1830, in Lambton County, Ont., where freed slaves settled and enjoyed the Dawn of Liberty.

'Let the tail go with the hide'.

An old saying from Prince Edward Island.

The seed from pumpkins are most commonly thrown away: but abundance of an excellent oil may be extracted from them. This oil burns well, gives a lively light and emits very little smoke.

'Cobourg Star and Newcastle General Advertiser'. (About 1800).

Battle of the Plains of Abraham. *The Public Archives of Canada.*

OUR GRASS ROOTS

A museum honours the tough warm-hearted breed of Cape Breton mining men, who since 1670, when Capt. Poulet first found their coal, have been identified with the coal and steel industries of the royal island.

In 1672 a book by Nicholas Denys, published in France, mentions these coal discoveries. It took 25 years before the French found surface coal at Louisbourg; and until 1720 for a shaft to be sunk at Morien.

The unique Miners' Museum, a centennial project, is above an old coal mine in Glace Bay, Cape Breton Island. Visitors descend into the bona fide mine, protected by the traditional gear, including a miner's hat and lamp.

In 1893 when the World's Fair was held at Chicago, wheat from the Peace River Valley won the championship. The question that was asked by everybody there, and even by the newspaper men covering the story, was 'Where is Peace River?'

SEAL LIVER
Sauté in butter till light brown, then cut in 2"x2" pieces. Add thinly sliced Arctic puff balls to about equal weight of liver. Place in buttered casserole, cover with whole milk (powdered or tinned). Bake fifteen minutes or till milk is thick.

'Poker is not a game but an education.' *Sir William Van Horne, 1920.*

SEPTEMBER

The first person to be executed officially in French Canada was a 16 year old female thief in 1649. A criminal escaped death by acting as her executioner.

However, Michel Gaillon, a companion of Roberval, was hanged in the winter of 1542-3 at Cap Rouge, (Charlesbourg Royal) – the first recorded (albeit unofficial) sentence of death.

The first hanging during the British regime in Kingston in 1788 was that of a man, later proved innocent, for stealing a watch.

Canada's last public execution was that of P. J. Whelan, assassin of Thomas D'Arcy McGee, 1869.

The last Public Execution.
The Public Archives of Canada.

DID YOU KNOW THAT

An Almanac of 1847 carried these two items:
Bethel School
Princes Street, Griffintown, Montreal.
R. Duncan and Mrs. Duncan, Teachers.
This school was erected in 1837, since which time 1,500 scholars have received gratuitous instruction, the daily average attendance is from 120 to 150.

On Sabbath-days there are religious services for seamen and emigrants, principally conducted by the Rev. Thaddeus Osgood.

Burlington Ladies' Academy
Hamilton, C.W.
Rev. D. C. Van Norman, A.M., Principal and Teacher of Natural Science, Moral and Mental Philosophy and Belles-Lettres.
Mrs. D. C. Van Norman, Preceptress and Teacher of Drawing, Painting, Perspective and Vocal Music.

The 'Telegram-Observer', an English-language weekly for the Eastern Townships, Quebec, which was started in 1869, printed its last issue on Sept. 9, 1965, almost a century later.

In 1872, ladies of Upper and Lower Canada, who could afford them, coveted gowns of silks, 'stiff enough to stand'. They paid eight and ten dollars a yard for the material, and even more for the lace trimming.

'His devotion to Canada and the Empire was steadfast and enduring.'
Inscription on monument in Central Park, Calgary, to Richard Bedford Bennett, Prime Minister of Canada, 1930-35.

OLD TIMOTHY

'More I lissen to folks' troubles, more I see that on'y jes' the names change, the stories are alwuz the same.'

Acorn Soup
Make in fall when acorns are ripe, grinding them between rocks. Fan the acorns with a fanning basket, to which the fine parts will stick. Put the fine meal in a wooden bin. Pour warm water over it three or four times to take out the bitter taste. Put acorn meal and water in a cooking basket (made with roots). Drop in a very hot rock. Keep turning the rock with a wooden spoon. Sometimes one rock will cook the soup.

DATES OF INTEREST

September 1617
The first marriage in Canada took place at Quebec between Stephen Jonquest and Anne Hébert, with Father Le Caron officiating.

September 1783
United Empire Loyalists wintered in Canada, before settling on their grants.

September 1818
The Earl of Selkirk was tried in Sandwich for breaking into Fort William and resisting arrest.

The sapphire, the September birthstone, is the symbol of truth, sincerity and faithfulness. The ancient Persians believed the earth rested on a sapphire whose reflection gave colour to the sky.

Canadians have celebrated Labour Day for a long time on the first Monday of September, although it was only in 1894 that it was declared as a statutory federal holiday for that date.

The Indians have at least two names for September – 'The Hunting Moon' and 'Nimituhumoowepesim' or 'The Moon – When – The – Deer Rub – Their – Horns'.

SEPTEMBER

Dr. George Mercer Dawson. 1849 – 1901. The Public Archives of Canada.

DID YOU KNOW THAT

From the 54th to the 60th parallel.

Dr. George Mercer Dawson, Canada's greatest geologist, predicted in 1870 that Northwest British Columbia would some day support five million people. Now the word is that the City of Dawson Creek is destined to become the cultural, financial, educational, medical and distribution centre of the 'sleeping giant of the northland.'

The greats and the near-greats are to be found at the Rideau Club, Wellington Street, Ottawa, which opened its doors in Sept. 1865. John A. Macdonald, George-Etienne Cartier and George Brown were among the founders. They felt the need for a comfortable club where they could forget the crude streets of Bytown, as Ottawa was then called. The men kept it to themselves until 1934, when they decided that ladies might be invited – in the evenings.

Henry Ellis, who later became governor of Nova Scotia, made a voyage of exploration to Hudson Bay, 1746-47. He noted that Indians and English alike used a plant called Wizzekapukka in 'nervous and scorbutick Disorders', to aid digestion and cause appetite.

Cowboy's Stew (not guaranteed to please):
2 gallons slough water
6 large onions, other vegetables if available
1 pound, or more, sowbelly (bacon)
3, 4, 5 or 6 wild ducks.
The Balance brings
Autumnal fruits,
The Scorpion stings,
The Archer shoots.

DATES OF INTEREST

September 17, 1792
At the election of a speaker at Parliament, there was discussion as to the language of the House being English or French. J. A. Panet, who favoured French, was elected speaker, 28 to 18.

September 19, 1654
Marguerite Sedilot, the youngest bride in Canadian records was married, aged 11 years and 5 mos., to Jean Aubuchon, of Three Rivers, Quebec. The ceremony was not validated until her twelfth birthday.

September 20, 1697
France recovered Acadia.

September 20, 1816
A stage began to run from York to Niagara.

September 20, 1898
Main portion of New Westminster, B.C. destroyed by fire, with damage of $2,000,000.

September 22, 1877
Treaty No. Seven or the Blackfoot Treaty was signed. The Indians surrendered 50,000 square miles in Southwest Alberta. A memorial on the reservation reads – 'Peace forever. In loving memory of Head Chief Red Crow. Born 1830. Died 1900, Signed Treaty No. 7, 1877. His successor Head Chief Crop Eared Wolf. Born 1846. Died 1913. And all who rest here.'

Everybody knows that neither praying nor grumbling pulls the cart from the mire; the sure way is to set a shoulder to the wheel.'

'The Letters of Mephibosheth Stepsure' by Thomas McCulloch, 1821.

OLD TIMOTHY

'Ef a cowboy had to go in a hurry, he jes took a ranch hawss. Nobody worrit. They knew the hawss would be sent back.'

'I know of no bird or animal that can equal the Canada Goose for getting well after being wounded. It is said that a cat has nine lives; if that is true, the Canada Goose has at least eighteen, nine on each side of the border.'
Jack Miner, O.B.E.

SEPTEMBER

Cheek music, or mouth music is what folks had to resort to when they got together for a dance but could find no fiddle, mouth organ or banjo. They made their own music by singing as they danced, and if the old-time lively steps left them short of breath, those who sat around kept things going by stamping out the rhythm.

In the 19th century, the waltz, quadrille, lancers and minuet were popular in the towns of Nova Scotia, but in the rural areas, folks liked the livelier dodging-six, strip-the-willow, clog, old barnyard eight (known as 'one to make the feet fly'), jigs, and the step-dance known as 'chicken-scratch'.

They must be joking when they speak of selling refrigerators to the Eskimos in the new villages of the Arctic circle. They have something as good, if not better, at their feet. They have only to make a hole in the permafrost beneath their topsoil to store caribou, salmon, char or anything else. Not only does the food freeze in a matter of hours, but it seems to keep perfectly and for very long periods. ◠ ◠

The name Ottawa, of Indian origin, has many fantastic interpretations, such as – 'short ears', 'long ears', 'hair put up', 'traders', 'men of the woods', and 'they boil', referring to the river rapids.

W. G. Edwards Sawmill . Rockland . before 1880.

The Public Archives of Canada

Six-foot-three, two-hundred-pound John Ware had a history of slavery behind him, but took at once to the beauty and freedom of the old west, where they still remember his horsemanship. He was not only respected, but loved by all who knew him in the 1880's.

The always cheerful negro had a bit of the showman about him, and always started by pretending he couldn't ride all that well, and then proceeded to do the most amazing things in the saddle. Trailing the herds for years, he would pick the meanest bronc in the corral, saying 'Think I'll ride that one.' No horse ever threw wild, huge, but quick-moving Black John. The 'Macleod Gazette' of June 23, 1885 said, 'The horse is not running on the prairie which John cannot ride, sitting with his face either to the head or tail, or even if the animal chooses to stand on its head or lie on its back. John always appears to be on top when the horse gets up, and smiling as if he enjoyed it.'

The Blackfoot Indians called him Sax-a-nap-i-can (black-white man) and their Chief Crowfoot, sensing a personality as unique as his own, did everything he could to persuade Black John to join his tribe.

He was so popular that the ranchers, of more recent years, used his name for the John Ware Society, a group formed to record the pioneer qualities on the prairies.

His own herd with the brand 9999 (4 nines) prospered but he was killed at 65 ironically when a very gentle horse fell on him. The Ware house near the Bow River, Alberta, was moved in 1958 to become a museum in Steveville Dinosaur Park.

OUR GRASS ROOTS

The first paper mill in Canada was established in 1805 in the little village of St. Andrews, near Lachute, Quebec. Its output was mainly wrapping and printing papers which were sold to local merchants and publishers. Rags were used and converted by hand methods into paper.

The first paper-making machine was in a mill built near Toronto, in 1826.

In the days when buffalo roamed near Fort Macleod in the N.W.T., the Indians drove them through a three-mile ravine between perpendicular rocks. Bones still cover the ground, where they were forced to death over the steep cliffs.

Archaeologists digging recently at Spring Point, Alberta, in a buffalo jump, found some knives and buffalo bones about 2,500 years old. The findings at this site reveal spear and arrow points, bone smashers, hide scrapers, drills, awls, pottery, and bake ovens. ◠ ◠

In the old days, if an Indian was killed by a white man, the red men avenged his death not necessarily by attacking the killer but by taking the life of any white man.

September

In 1899 seven cast iron stoves bought for $29.50 each in Vancouver were sold in the N.W.T. near Macleod for $250 a piece.

❦ ❦

In the pioneer days, with no doctors available, women had many remedies using nature's fruits. Tea made of wild cherry and dogwood bark was a cure-all. Sunflower seeds infused in a home-brew liquor for 12 hours, or more, was held to cure rheumatism if drunk every night for seven nights. Almost every medicine was made with whisky or home-brew and taken liberally for snakebite or pains in the joints.

The Blackfoot were an important union of three Algonkian-speaking Indian tribes, of southern Alberta and northern Montana – the Blackfoot, Piegan and the Blood. The name Blackfoot is from dark smears of ashes on their moccasins. Their own name for themselves is 'Siksika'.

'Family trees are apt to be questionable about the roots.'
Sir William Van Horne.

An excellent recipe for longevity is this — cultivate a minor ailment, and take very good care of it.
Attributed to Sir William Osler.

The Public Archives of Canada.

Chinese more than any other race were responsible for building the historic Canadian Pacific Railway across the Rockies. Theirs was the hardest labour – through the punishing canyons and the back-breaking mountain passes.

● ●

Butter at 50 cts. a lb. is thought cheap in Victoria, B.C.

There are no five-cent pieces in B.C. The lowest piece is a 'bit' or 10 cts.

A lot of Russian Lutherans are to settle in Manitoba next spring.

Port Perry, Ont. has set villages a good example by organizing an efficient fire brigade.

Concrete houses are being introduced into Toronto.

The Mennonites in Manitoba build bake ovens of clay, which extend through both the kitchen and 'drawing room.'

The first pile at the entrance of False Bay Lake, Mira Bay, Cape Breton County, was driven on Aug. 29, and the work of turning the lake into an artificial harbour 'Port Hiawatha' is proceeding.

The 'Family Herald and Weekly Star', Sept. 16, 1876.

OUR GRASS ROOTS

Improvisation of a most unusual order was introduced to bring out the 'Macleod Gazette' in Alberta, in 1886. There were all sorts of difficulties in getting the plant together, but finally everything was pretty much in order except that the engine had not been installed in the cylinder press from Fort Benton. How to get the paper out was solved by lining up a dozen Indian braves at the handle of the press. As each warrior grew exhausted from turning the heavy press, another stepped into his place until the whole edition was printed.

In 1648, when Jacques Boisson, of Quebec, was licensed as the first innkeeper, it was with the understanding that he sell no liquor while religious services were being held.

❦ ❦

A French soldier encountered some Wyandotte Indians in the 1600's and thought their cropped bristly hair was very much like the boars in his native forests. He called them Hurons, from the old French word 'hure' meaning 'bristles of the boar.'

❦ ❦

By pure chance, archaeologists turned up French commemorative medals, dated 1720, in the ruins of the Louisbourg fortress on Cape Breton Island. They were found in the King's Bastion, during the restoration of the massive fortifications which were begun by the French about 250 years ago to defend the sea passage to the Gulf of St. Lawrence.
The capture of Louisbourg in 1758 was a prelude to the British capture of Quebec.

❦ ❦

DATES OF INTEREST

September 25, 1810
The first issue of **The Kingston Gazette**, a weekly, was brought out. There were two earlier papers in Upper Canada, **The Upper Canada Gazette** at Newark in 1793 and **The York Gazette** in 1801.

September 28, 1663
An edict forbids selling or giving liquor to Indians.

Respected British Columbia oldtimers included W. A. Cumyow, a court interpreter of the 1860's, Goon Ling Dang, a merchant who came to Victoria in 1877 and Yip Sang, a paymaster for the C.P.R. at Yale, in 1882. Montrealers recall 6 foot 3 Rev. Nam Sing Chan, the tallest man in Chinatown, born in 1880. He spent 22 years as the first minister at the Chinese Presbyterian Church on Chenneville Street where a Jewish Synagogue used to be. The story is told of how he used to carry a sick Chinese on his back to a doctor or nursing home. His son Rev. Paul S. Chan serves the same congregation. Other old Montrealers included court interpreter Wong Him and merchant Wong Foo.

The Public Archives of Canada.

The Right Honourable Sir Wilfrid Laurier, has had at least twenty places named in his honour. Laurier Township and Laurier Lake, in Ontario; Laurier Mountain in the Yukon Territory; an 11,750 mountain peak in British Columbia and the Laurier River of the Mackenzie district are but a few.

Among the gentilities of life, visits hold a prominent place and deserve attention. The time is twelve o'clock noon; before that hour the lady of the house is supposed to be busy at her household duties. Occupy but a brief time in your call . . . if strongly urged to remain longer it would be impolite to go in haste, but let 15 or 20 minutes be the time spent in the visit.

Never look about you in a room, as if you were taking inventory.

When invited to dinner, avoid arriving either too early or too late. In either case it is rudeness, in the former you inconvenience your hostess in the latter her guests.

New Brunswick Almanac, 1865.

Branding, whipping, hanging and deportation to the galleys of France were common punishment of New France.

Perjurers were branded on the tongue. Military deserters were marked with the letter 'D' and then deported. Usually the branding was held in the open, with the prisoner in irons. A red-hot iron, bearing a Crown device burnt the culprit's palm, during the time he took to say 'God Save the King' three times.

About 1681, unlicensed coureurs de bois, were branded for the first offense. For the second they were sent to the galleys of France for life.

DID YOU KNOW THAT

Alumni, among the old and beautiful trees on the campus of McGill University in Montreal, paused sentimentally at the Founder's Elm, thought to be 200 years old, which was but a seedling during the late days of James McGill's life.

Then they wandered past maples, lindens and horse chestnuts to pay respects to one of the most famous campus landmarks, the Ginkgo tree, which boasted a 300 million-year ancestry, at the site of the tomb of James McGill, in front of the old Arts Building. No longer can this ritual be followed, for the Gingko tree is gone. Stricken by a mysterious malady, in 1966 it had to be cut down in sections and taken away.

This fine old tree arrived in 1904 as a gift from Japan in appreciation of a visit from Dr. David P. Penhallow, the first appointed Professor of Botany at McGill University. He had spent 1902-1903 as a visiting professor at Zezo (the old name for Hokkaido) in Japan, and became interested in conifers.

Only a few of this ancient species survived the glacial period. They were saved from extinction by Chinese holy men who planted them in sacred temple gardens, a custom followed by the Japanese.

The Eskimo, fishing for arctic char today, follows tradition and uses pretty much the same type of spear as did his forbears. Equipped with the fish spear which he had made during the winter, of musk-ox prongs bound to a wooden handle with sealskin thongs, the Eskimo leaves his camp at the height of the brief arctic summer and moves upstream to an ancestral fishing site on the Sapotit River. A good catch means winter food for the Eskimo families and their dogs. Eaten raw, they consider the fish a great delicacy.

Mr. Latham, surgeon to the King's Regiment of Foot, entered into inoculation (of small-pox) to be of use to mankind. All poor may apply to Mr. Latham, who will inoculate, attend and give medicine gratis. Mr. L. practises midwifery. For the cautious: he designs to inoculate his daughter, a child between two and three years. The Battery, Upper Town.
The Quebec 'Gazette', Sept. 1768.

'Arrived this day at the canyon at 10 a.m. and drowned running the canoe down. God bless my poor wife.'

J. Carpenter, of Toronto, an Overlander going to the Cariboo, B.C., diary, Sept. 30, 1862, before losing his life in the rapids at Grand Canyon, Fraser River.

AUTUMN

OCTOBER

A View of the City of Quebec, by H. Smyth.   *Public Archives of Canada.*

DID YOU KNOW THAT

A few miles from downtown Toronto, one steps back a century at Pioneer Village, Black Creek Conservation Area, Canada West, a typical crossroads settlement of south central Ontario as it was before 1867. Standing as originally constructed are churches, the squire's house, log houses, smoke rooms, herb gardens, farms, tool sheds, blacksmith and wheelwright shops, emporiums and artisan's quarters, all with much to see inside and out.

Excellent recipes from 1832-67, served by the Canadian National Institute for the Blind, might include Scotch beef stew with dumplings and hot slaw; fried sausages with sauerkraut and pumpkin pie; pressed chicken, cucumber salad and shoo-fly pie; Dutch hot potato salad, knackwurst, and corn fritters with maple syrup and raw potato pancakes with apple sauce, fastnachts, blitzkuchen and strudel all coming hot from the kitchen.

Right now, in the fall, is the best time for the angler who wants to get a maskinonge; and if he's lucky he might get one that weighs a good seventy pounds. For this, he will need plenty of stamina, for the maskinonge is known as the 'ferocious fighter of the fresh waters.'

This fish goes by a great variety of names – muskallunge, muscalonge, muscallonge, and muskellunge. It is even called pike, but, never, never perch-pike. Around the Great Lakes, the English-speaking people call it simply 'lunge' and dream of getting one.

The name is derived from the Indian name for the fish, in its French spelling. 'Maskinonge' is its name in the statutes of Canada and of the provinces of Quebec and Ontario.

Drawing and painting were a required part of a good education in the old days, and it is well for our archives that this was so, for military personnel, officials and their wives, teachers, missionaries and explorers created a graphic record of a Canada that has vanished forever.

Associates of the Hudson's Bay Company and members of the Royal North West Mounted Police left illustrated chronicles which enrich our museums and libraries. Paul Kane, in his great trek of 1846, made over five hundred sketches of the west. Artists were with Palliser's Expedition in 1857. Ernest Thompson Seton was another who depicted the North West and William G. R. Hind recorded with his pencil and brush the exciting story of the gold-seeking Overlanders in 1862. British and European newspapers sent their staff artists to transmit studies of Canada to their interested eager readers.

It is not possible to overestimate the value of the contributions made by C. W. Jefferys, R.C.A., LL.D., (1869-1951), Canada's foremost historical artist; William Notman (1826-1891), the brilliant photographer; Henri Octave Julien (1852-1908) the remarkable cartoonist, illustrator and painter, and others of this genre.

Treasured documents also include works by Sgt. Reckitt ('Fort Walsh in 1880'); Const. Elroy ('Taking the Guns Through the Dirt Hills in 1870'); and a drawing by Lawson of the Manitoba 'Free Press' ('Fort Qu'Appelle in 1867').

'. . . The safety of the French race is not in isolation but in the struggle. Give our children the best education possible, put them on a footing of equality with those of the other race, and give them the legitimate pride which they will have in such a struggle. There is safety . . .'

Laurier, 1896.

OCTOBER

The Quebec Bridge. *The Public Archives of Canada.*

DATES OF INTEREST

October 1, 1876
The first shipment of wheat was sent out of the Canadian West. 857$\frac{1}{16}$ bushels went to Ontario for seed, for there the wheat crop had been unsuccessful. Twelve farmers furnished the grain, some of it weighing 64 pounds to the bushel.

October 2, 1758
The first representative government in Canada met in Halifax Court House.

October 7, 1690
The annual fete of Notre Dame de la Victoire commemorates the defeat of the British invaders under General Phips at Quebec. The historic little church of the same name, still standing in Quebec's Lower Town, dates from 1688, and is supposed to be the oldest church in Canada, next to the Basilica in Quebec. Partially destroyed during Wolfe's seige in 1759, it was rebuilt on the old walls.

October 8, 1804
The Government schooner 'Speedy', and all her passengers, lost on Lake Ontario.

OUR GRASS ROOTS

The magnificent Quebec Bridge was completed in 1917, but not without two dreadful disasters. It was designed as the world's largest cantilever bridge to go over the St. Lawrence, just six miles above Quebec City and started in 1900. When it was near completion in 1907, one of the cantilever spans collapsed, carrying 75 workmen to their death in the river below. When the bridge was almost at completion a second time, the centre span fell into the river, and this time 13 men were killed. In all, 88 lives were given for this structure.

When Eugene O'Keefe and two partners went into the brewing business in Toronto in 1862, beer at twenty cents a gallon was a staple at mealtimes. Food on the table was plentiful, too, for chickens were forty cents a pair, and a side of beef came at four cents a pound.

The partners developed the Hannath and Hart Brewery, built in 1840, which became known as the O'Keefe Company. On Oct. 1, 1960, the 12.5 million dollar O'Keefe Centre for the Performing Arts opened its doors – a contribution to Toronto's cultural life.

The Last of the Beothuks.
Because of his interest in the Beothuks, the Indian aborigines of Newfoundland, explorer William Epps Cormack kept Nancy Shanawdithit, the last known survivor, in his home until her death in 1829, to obtain information about the tribe.

His interest had been excited seven years before when he spent nine weeks crossing Newfoundland on foot, the first white man to make that trip. Cabot had left notes of the ochre and red paint which the Beothuks used, and it is thought that the term 'redskin' or 'red Indian' came from this custom.

OLD TIMOTHY

'No pioneer ever turned folks (white or red) away without food. Tea wuz hoarded fer callers, an' a pound would be stretched out to last a whole year.'

The opal, which is the symbol of hope, and the tourmaline, which exhilarates the spirit, are the birthstones for October. Queen Victoria gave each of her daughters opals on their wedding days.

Indians call October 'The Falling Leaf Moon' and also 'Pimuhumoowepesim' or 'The Migrating Moon'.

OCTOBER

'For a long time there have been complaints that the education given in our seminaries does not fully correspond to the needs of the century, that it is too much turned toward the study of ancient languages and old theories.'

'*Le Canadien*', 1836. *(trans.)*

Proud as the sod-busters are of Saskatchewan, they enjoy many a quip about the 'Pion-era'. They like to tell of the gay nineties when the party men were all gay and the women all ninety.

Louis XV of France marked the loss of Quebec to the British with a magnificent dinner, happy that there would no longer be such 'an alarming drain on the treasury.' Voltaire sent a congratulatory message to His Highness because he had 'rid himself of those fifteen thousand arpents of snow.'

When the luckless Montcalm, carried to a convent, heard his wound was mortal, he said 'So much the better, I shall not see the surrender of Quebec.' To De Ramezay, he said, 'To your keeping I commend the honour of France; as for me, I shall pass the night with God and prepare myself for death.'

OLD TIMOTHY

'Settlers have their own way of deciding what's important. Their rating goes something like this – Old Timers, the Holy Family, and the Royal Family.'

To stop a nose bleed roll up and press a piece of paper under the upper lip. In obstinate cases blow a little gum Arabic powder up the nostrils through a quill, which will immediately stop the discharge. Powdered alum is also good.

'Nova Scotia is an excellent poor man's country, because almost any man, in any walk of industry, by perseverance and economy, can secure the comforts of life.'

Joseph Howe, July 31, 1834.

DATES OF INTEREST

October 9, 1877
First locomotive at Winnipeg.

October 9, 1891
Corner-stone laid of English church, Knowlton, Que.

October 11, 1869
Half-breeds, under Louis Riel, compelled surveyor Webb to cease his work in Manitoba.

October 10, 1864
A conference of delegates met in Quebec; from this resulted the Confederation of Canada.

October 13, 1812
Brilliant and audacious Sir Isaac Brock, the 'heart and soul' of the defence of Upper Canada in the War of 1812, defeated the American invaders on the Niagara frontier, but was mortally wounded. Gazetted a K.C.B. three days before his death, the news did not arrive while he was still alive. In 1824, the foundation stone of a monument to Brock was laid with full Masonic honours, with Wm. Lyon Mackenzie participating actively, and placing a copy of his **Advocate** in the hollow stone. Sir Peregrine Maitland ordered it removed, and Mackenzie complied. But more excitement was to come, for sixteen years later, Lett, a renegade Canadian, blew up the monument. However, in 1841, 8,000 people met with Sir George Arthur at the ruined memorial to pledge restoration at public expense.

OUR GRASS ROOTS

Paul Bunyan once built a new type of sawmill. The saw stood still while the mill turned, and it proved to be a tremendous success. It made so much sawdust that there was no lumber to pile; and thus effected a great saving in labor. When Johnny Inkslinger had figured out the profits, he was so amazed that he stood transfixed for three days on one leg in the office doorway, gazing at the mill in astonishment. He stood there so long that his books got out of balance, and the Department of Internal Revenue sent a squad to find what was wrong. The revenue men found that the Excise tax on the snuce hadn't been paid. That was the end of Paul Bunyan. He and Johnny Inkslinger had to hit out for the North Woods to avoid being jugged for tax aversion and they ain't been back since.

'*Bridge River – Lillooet News*', 1945. *Paul Bunyan is forever thinking up new ways of doing things.*

PROCLAMATION.
Province of Upper Canada.

ISAAC BROCK, Esquire, President administering the Government of the Province of Upper Canada, and Major-General commanding His Majesty's Forces within the same.

TO ALL TO WHOM IT MAY CONCERN – GREETING.

WHEREAS information has been received, that divers persons have recently come into this Province, with a seditious intent to disturb the tranquility thereof...

GIVEN under my Hand and Seal, at Arms, at York this Twenty-fourth day of February...

ISAAC BROCK, President.

'Valour gave them a common death,
History a common fame,
Posterity a common monument.'

Translation from the Latin, of an inscription on the obelisk back of the Chateau Frontenac, Quebec City, which was erected to the memory of Generals Wolfe and Montcalm in 1827 by Lord Dalhousie. James Thompson, the last survivor of Wolfe's Army, who took part in the capture of 1759, laid the cornerstone at the age of 95.

It was Sir Louis Hippolyte Lafontaine, who in 1849, successfully sponsored a bill before the Legislature of the United Canadas, to abolish imprisonment for debt. But not before much hardship had been endured in both Lower and Upper Canada by debtors. This was so under the French régime in the 17th century, and even more so under British rule in the 18th. In some areas, the debtor was allowed 'bail' to walk about in a carefully limited district, but in no way was he able to earn money to pay off his debts.

The Public Archives of Canada.

They called him 'Non-pareil'.
He lifted a platform with 4 horses, weighing 4,100 lbs.; placed a barrel of cement on his shoulder with one hand and picked up 551 lbs. with one finger. Strong man Louis Cyr was born in Lower Canada on Oct. 10, 1863 but took his 5 foot, 10½ inch tall, 365 lb. body to many contests in Europe.

In England in 1892, the Marquess of Queensberry challenged him to hold to a standstill a pair of hitched driving horses headed in opposite directions. He did – and drove the horse given him as a prize proudly, when he returned to Montreal. When at 29, he defeated the strong men of Europe before 1500 people in London's Aquarian Hall, his huge girth was ornamented by the diamond-studded World's Champion Police Gazette Belt.

The eight-foot giant Edouard Beaupré, of Saskatchewan, cried like a baby when 'Non-pareil' defeated him. A friendlier adversary was Father Labelle, another legendary strong man, known also as 'the apostle of colonization.'

His athletic feats left Cyr dissatisfied. What he wanted above all thing was to be a violinist.

That the immigrants missed their English gardens is shown by this 1836 letter sent overseas – 'Do not forget to enclose flower seeds and the stones of plums, damsons, bullace, pips of the best kinds of apples, nuts from the old Spanish nut trees, seeds of our wild primrose, sweet violet and lucerne-seed.' (Bullace is a type of plum or damson, and lucerne a variation of purple medic or alfalfa)

Out west a corn dance is part of the Thanksgiving harvest celebration. Everybody hopes to find an ear with red kernels, for that betokens a happy love life.

The first bit of British trading for furs took place on a ship. The 40-ton ketch NONSUCH under the patronage of King Charles II, of England, dropped anchor in Hudson's Bay in 1668. The crew of 42 constructed a tiny log trading post right on the ketch to accomodate the Indians and Eskimos who started to bring furs aboard. They named the post Fort Charles in honour of the monarch.

DID YOU KNOW THAT

Everybody knows the famous painting of 'The Founders of Canada'. Our government, in 1883, commissioned Robert Harris to paint it for $4000, showing the 34 delegates who attended the historic meeting in Quebec City in 1864. The painting was unfortunately destroyed in the disastrous fire in the Parliament Building in Ottawa where it was hanging. The artist did not feel he could undertake painting the Confederation scene again, but presented to the government his original full-size charcoal sketch.
It may be seen in the House of Commons.

'Emigrate ye Canadians! If England will not treat you with decency, shake the dust from your feet, cross the border and build up a home where tyranny does not dare show its head'.

Cincinnati 'News', quoted in Cobourg 'Plain Speaker'.

Differing from Whitewood, which was settled by the French nobility, but still aristocratic, was Cannington Manor in Sasketchewan, at a small siding of the newly-built C.P.R. that was later to be known as Moosomin.

It started in the 1880's when Captain Pierce, an Englishman, arrived. So well did he like what he saw, he went to Prime Minister John A. Macdonald to discuss his plans. He intended to publish a letter in the London **Times**, telling people **of his own class** that it was possible to establish a real English settlement on the prairies and live like lords on money that in England would be eaten up by taxes and rates.

He must have written a convincing letter, for everything went as he hoped. Before long, Cannington Manor saw Englishmen riding to hounds, breeding race horses, bowling on the cricket greens and happy at tennis. There were strawberry lawn parties, or they called upon one another at tea time to be served from a silver teapot. Thin bread and butter and English pound cake were taken for granted in this settlement 40 miles from a railroad. Before long, a Turf Club was formed in 1889. In the time that could be spared from the racing stables and dog kennels, men tried their hand at farming.

Cannington Manor was a fine mansion of many rooms, among them a ball room, gun room, gaming hall, sewing boudoir — all as much as possible like what the Pierce family had enjoyed in England. Beautiful crystal chandeliers illuminated the chambers. There is no doubt that the colony left its mark on Saskatchewan, and the old settlement is being reconstructed as an historic site.

OCTOBER

At the time of the Gold Rush of 1898, the motto of the Yukon Order of Pioneers was 'Do unto others as you would they should do unto you.' No man starved if any man had food. The unwritten law was that a man could walk into any cabin on the trail in the owner's absence and help himself to food and lodging. No door was locked. But he must leave an adequate supply of kindling, lay a fire ready in the stove and clean up. Another rule was that a prospector making a strike must spread the news to everyone he met.

There are 'scrapbook Hansards' which are simply clippings of Parliament proceedings before 1875 when Canadian Hansard came out in printed form.

'Governor of the Arctic Circle.'
That was what they called RCMP Commissioner Stuart Taylor Wood, C.M.G., who was stationed at Herschel Island in the 1920's. RCMP historians say that the period in which he served the force so well was one of extreme activity and responsibility.

He came by his experience naturally, for his father Zachary Taylor Wood was in command of the Royal North West Mounted Police that kept such splendid order in the Yukon during the Gold Rush.

**'Of the black bear, you need not be afraid,
But killing white ones is a dangerous trade.'** *Eskimo saying.*

The Palace Grand, the most lavish entertainment centre during the Gold Rush. The Public Archives of Canada.

At various times, 'un écu' of New France was worth anywhere from sixty cents to one dollar.

'For permanent Peace by the help of God let us build more Friendships instead of Warships.'

Jack Miner, O.B.E.

By Tory now is understood
A man who seeks his country's good.
Definition of the United Empire Loyalists in 1777.

I have generally seen that **bundling** is not the short road to marriage.

'Letters of Mephibosheth Stepsure' by Thomas McCulloch, 1821.

DATES OF INTEREST

October 18, 1759
The British fleet left Quebec for England. The embalmed remains of Gen. Wolfe went home on the 'Royal William'.

October 20, 1889
Warburton Pike said, in the Northwest, 'I cannot believe that the herds of buffalo were larger than the throngs of caribou. Their passage of six days showed the numbers of these animals still roaming the Barrens.'

October 21, 1873
Powder mills exploded at Windsor mills, Quebec.

October 23, 1847
Sixty-five immigrants died in one week at Point St. Charles, Montreal. Almost ten thousand immigrants died in 1847.

DID YOU KNOW THAT

Everybody in Saskatchewan knew and respected the Métis Gabriel Lavallie, who until his death in 1959, told eye-witness stories of almost 100 years of life, hunting the buffalo, scouting at Fort Walsh and homesteading in the Cypress Hills. The son of Louis Lavallie, also an intrepid scout, he traced his ancestry through his grandmother Julia Mackenzie back to Sir Alexander Mackenzie, of Arctic fame. As a child he played games with bullets he dug out of dead buffalo.

If you look at a map of the Maritime Provinces you will see that Nova Scotia missed being an island because of the Isthmus of Chignecto, which at its narrowest is only seventeen miles across. Diego Homen, a Portuguese, who voyaged into Chignecto waters in 1558, drew the first map of the Basin.

Because they had 'a taste for freedom', a group of 300 negro people left Oklahoma and walked the long miles to Amber Valley, near Athabaska, a few years after Alberta became a province. Clearing the timber they farmed successfully. The community has an elementary and high school, where at one time only four of the enrollment of fifty were white.

'Potlatch' is a Chinook jargon word meaning 'a giving away.' It is thought of as a status symbol, for the chief who ended up without any possessions enjoyed the highest prestige. All of this is true, but just a bit of an over-simplification. Anthropologists who have studied the Indians of the North Pacific Coast, point out that the guests who were showered with lavish, costly gifts and succulent food knew very well that before long the guest would be host to the chief giving the potlatch.

There are songs from ancient days making clear that the potlatch was a kind of fighting, a making of war, but with property instead of death-dealing devices. This old song of the Kwakiutl and Koskimo Indians tells of the eighteen-day winter dance ceremonial at Fort Rupert in 1895: 'Instead of fighting our enemies with his death bringer, we fight with these blankets and other kinds of property . . . Of olden times the Kwakiutl ill treated my forefathers and fought them so that the blood ran over the ground. Now we fight with button blankets and other kinds of property, smiling at each other. Oh, how good is the new time! We used to fight with bows and arrows, with spears and guns . . . Now, we fight with copper, and if we have no coppers, we fight with canoes or blankets.'

OCTOBER

In the 1890's, at a big political meeting in the Foothills, the Hon. Sir Clifford Sifton asked whether there was anyone in the hall who was not a Liberal. A little old Scotch-Canadian said, 'I'm a Conservative.' Sifton went on, 'How do you feel, the only Conservative in this big hall full of Liberals?' The old man answered, 'Like a grain of Manitoba No. 1 hard wheat in a bin full of what the rats left behind.'

Chairs were seldom found in the homes of early settlers. Usually benches, seating from two to six people, were near the open hearth.

Hon. Clifford Sifton, M.P. — The Public Archives of Canada.

OUR GRASS ROOTS

He was a man who knew just how to get on with the natives, from the very first day that he started out as a pedlar with a pack on his back. For John Jacob Astor, born in Germany in 1763, made it the hard way.

It was the Jay Treaty of 1794 that gave him a real push forward. The British Government had stopped the direct export of furs from Canada to the States, after the English colonies had revolted. Furs had to be shipped from Montreal to England and the continent; and then came the expense and hazards of another trip back to the United States. The Jay Treaty allowed furs to go directly from Canada to the United States.

Astor said, 'Now the fur trade will build me a fortune.' It did. He became the richest man in America, with assets estimated at 20 million dollars.

On an autumn day in 1827, he sold 200,000 muskrats publicly and 350,000 privately – 'so many have never in the world been sold in one day.' They brought him about 36 cents each, and his stock still included 200,000 peltries. It seems to add up to about one quarter of a million dollars right there.

Very little schooling was given to Silas Tertius Rand, one of twenty-two children. Born in 1810 at Cornwallis, Nova Scotia, he was apprenticed early to a bricklayer. However at twenty-four, he joined the Baptist ministry, and devoted his life to the Micmac Indians, as the first Protestant missionary to the Indians of Nova Scotia.

He showed a great gift for languages, and compiled a 40,000 word **Dictionary of the Language of the Micmac Indians** and translated the Bible into the Micmac tongue.

'Voluntary service is a boon to the individual and a blessing to the community.'
General George P. Vanier, D.S.O., M.C., C.D., LL.D., Governor-General of Canada 1959 to 1967.

'Our question is not what we would like to do, but what we can do.'
Joseph Howe, 1852.

'Thunderin' long words ain't wisdom.'
Justice Thomas Chandler Haliburton, c. 1853.

OLD TIMOTHY

'Folks on THE ISLAND usta say, 'Bad beginnins' make good endins'.'

Where did barter goods come from? 'The Fur Trade in Canada', by Harold A. Innis, lists these principal articles from Great Britain for the Indian trade-big business in 1781:

Blankets from Oxfordshire.
Strouds, coatings, moltons, serges and flannel, common blue and scarlet cloths, from Yorkshire.
Large quantities of hardware, brass, copper and tin kettles.
Indian fusils, pistols, powder, ball, shot and flints.
Painters' colors, vermillion etc.
Striped cottons, dimities, janes, fustians, shawls and handkerchiefs, gartering and ferreting, from Manchester.
Irish linens, large quantities of worsted yarn, threads, nets, twine, birdlime, Scotch sheetings.

Prices of goods at Fort des Prairies about the same time were:

A gun	20	beaver	skins.
A stroud blanket	10	,,	,,
A white blanket	8	,,	,,
An axe, of one pound weight	3	,,	,,
Half pint gunpowder	1	,,	,,
Ten balls	1	,,	,,

Principal profits accrued from the sale of knives, beads, flints, steels, awls and other small objects.

OCTOBER

For many centuries All-Hallows Even, All-Hallomas or All Saints' Day has been celebrated by children with broomsticks, pumpkins, nuts, apples, and mild – or not so mild – mischief. Here the 'trick or treat' holiday has taken on a new dimension since the Nobel Peace Prize was awarded to Unicef in 1965. As pirates, clowns, knights and fair ladies come to call, most homes have a bowl of silver coins for the Unicef box, and another bowl of goodies for the little fun-makers.

Field of Pumpkins. The Public Archives of Canada.

DID YOU KNOW THAT

This plaque on a bench outside the new Vanier Library at Loyola College, Montreal, was unveiled Oct. 27, 1964. A special room named after Thomas D'Arcy McGee is dedicated to the history of the Irish in Canada.

Lintel Stones
Carved with shamrocks
From the house given to
Thomas D'Arcy McGee
in 1864
On the south side of St. Catherine Street
Two doors east of Drummond Street
near the site of Loyola College
from 1898 to 1916
Where George P. Vanier was a student
and graduated in 1906.

DATES OF INTEREST

October 24, 1621
Abraham Martin, original owner of the historic Plains of Abraham, where the armies of Wolfe and Montcalm battled, became the father of a son, Eustache, the first white child of French descent to be born in Canada.

Dear Madame Albani-Gye,
   I am sending you with these lines the souvenir I spoke of when I wished you good-bye, in recollection of that charming evening of 18th Sept. which I shall always remember with pleasure. Trusting that you will have a good passage, and that your health may be good, and you not overtire yourself,
      Believe me always,
      Yours very sincerely,
   Victoria, R. I.
Balmoral Castle, Oct. 29, 1891.

   Although world fame came early to the prima donna, Emma Albani, who was born Marie Louise Emma Cécile Lajeunesse on a farm at Chambly, Quebec on Sept. 24, 1847, she died in comparative poverty. She was a favourite of Queen Victoria, who sent as 'souvenirs' mentioned in the above letter: – a beautiful pearl cross and necklace, a Coronation and a Jubilee portrait, and three small pictures of herself in a silver and enamel case with this card, 'I hear you always carry my photo when you travel. This will be more convenient.'

There were times when the Queen requested Madame Albani to sing nothing but Mendelssohn's songs for an hour or more, but usually she asked for favourites like – 'Caro Nome', 'Robin Adair', 'Ave Maria', 'Home Sweet Home', 'Bluebells of Scotland', 'Annie Laurie' and 'Within a Mile of Edinboro' Town'.

Saskatchewan was founded by immigrants, the traditions of each ethnic group making an imprint. There was the Cannington Manor of the English, the French settlements at Gravelbourg and Lafleche, the Elfros and Bjorkdale of the Iceland people, Veregin for the Doukhobor folk, Stuartburn and Tolstoi for the Ukranians and still others settlements at Blumenhoff, Esterhazy, Steinback, Lettonia, Herzl, Hirsch, Beaconsfield, Zangwill and Hoffer.

October 27, 1854
A passenger and gravel train collided on the Great Western Railway between Chatham and Windsor — 47 killed.

October 31, 1780
The 'Ontario', a new vessel with 16 guns, and the full crew and thirty men of the 34th regiment, were all lost on Lake Ontario.

About 45% of the free world's newspaper pages are printed on Canadian newsprint.

OCTOBER

In 1823, the residents of the Parish of Charleston, Hatley, Quebec, formed a society for the purpose of suppressing vice, counterfeiting, horse stealing and various kindred felonies

'There are those who think they pay me a compliment in saying I am just like a white woman. I am Indian, and my aim, my joy, my pride, is to sing the glories of my people.'

E. Pauline Johnson (Tekahionwake).

✤ ✤ ✤ ✤ ✤ ✤ ✤ ✤

'Whiskey drowns some troubles and floats a lot more.'

Bob (Chambers) Edwards, The *'Calgary Eye Opener'*, 1915.

'The value of experience is not in seeing much, but in seeing wisely.'
Sir William Osler, 'The Army Surgeon', 1905.

∽ ∽

Many of the Welsh people who settled in the N.W.T. in 1902 were descendents of those who had immigrated to Patagonia, South America, in 1865 and not found it to their liking. Saltcoats, Saskatchewan, was more what they wanted and before long these new farmers filled the land with their music and song.

∽ ∽

Dr Wilfred Grenfell. circa 1911. The Public Archives of Canada.

Canadian home-brewed ale, strong, brown, with a good cream, lay about in kegs . . . to be tossed off at a gulp in the hay fields; an old custom, for ancient drinking cups had round bottoms . . . and necessitated emptying at a single draught.

Ready to give your clocks the Daylight Saving Time treatment? Follow this thought:
　　Fall back
　　Spring forward.
The change occurs (where it does occur in Canada) the last Sunday in October.

OLD TIMOTHY

'Nobody worrit about a night on the plains. Alwuz had buffalo robes to fix 'under and over'. Better'n blankets, Buffalos have thick wool, not hair, and nothin' could be warmer.'

✤ ✤ ✤ ✤ ✤ ✤ ✤ ✤

The Labrador Doctor, Sir Wilfred Thomason Grenfell, a man of great energy and enthusiasm, used to inspire his Mission workers with the same qualities, by saying, 'Start something. Somebody else will always finish it.'

The Argonauts of 1862, or The Overlanders of '62, were names given to bands of young emigrants who left Eastern Canada for the overland journey to the Cariboo gold fields of British Columbia. Most of the men, numbering two hundred in all, settled on the west coast.

Susanna Moodie tells how she made 'excellent' coffee from dandelion roots, in the fall of 1835: 'I washed the roots . . . without depriving them of the fine brown skin, which contains the aromatic flavour so like coffee while roasting. I cut them the size of a kidney bean, and roasted them on a pan in the stove oven, until brown and crisp as coffee. I ground and transferred a cupful of the powder to the coffee-pot, pouring upon it scalding water and boiling it for a few minutes briskly. The result was beyond my expectations — far superior to the common coffee procured at the stores'.

OUR GRASS ROOTS

About 1650, we hear of the 'Confrérie de Sainte Anne', a guild of joiners and carpenters, led by Jean Le Vasseur. Honouring the patron saint of wood-workers, they built and decorated for their own services, the Sainte Anne Chapel in the First Quebec basilica. Guild members led an annual procession of Fête-Dieu.

These talented craftsmen were followed by many others from France, who devoted themselves to a tradition of architecture and wood carving that is still flourishing in Quebec.

Sacred vessels demanded fine gold and silversmiths and about 1700 Sieur Saint-Paul Lambert was unique. His mark – P.L. under a madonna lily – is sought·by collectors, for his work is similar to that of Paul Revere, of American fame.

✤ ✤ ✤ ✤ ✤ ✤ ✤ ✤ ✤ ✤

NOVEMBER

OUR GRASS ROOTS

All through the summer of 1885, the work of laying steel for the Canadian Pacific Railway went steadily on, each stage of the work a triumph over the handicaps of the terrain. Now it was finished. The last span was fitted into place.

No golden spike for Donald A. Smith! He considered the plain iron one that Roadmaster F. A. Brothers fitted into place as a better augury for long service and prosperity . . . Donald Smith was a little excited . . . he struck the spike sideways instead of driving it home. The Roadmaster . . . set another in its place . . . The hammer was raised . . . The **last spike had been driven!** *Julie C. Crawford, Craigellachie, B.C., November 7, 1885.*

On Nov. 1, 1697, long before Newfoundland and Quebec were snatching at Labrador, the whole territory was granted to Joseph de la Penja (Penha), a Jewish merchant of Rotterdam, by William III, King of England, Scotland, France, Netherlands and Ireland and Prince of Orange, to mention only a few of his titles of authority. The original document is in the American Jewish Archives in Cincinnati, Ohio.

Although no member of the de la Penha family settled in the virtually inaccessible area, the grant was renewed in 1732 and 1768. After extensive litigation in the 1920's and 30's, during which a descendant, Rabbi Isaac de la Penha, of the Spanish and Portuguese Synagogue, in Montreal, put forth his claim, the Privy Council established the rights of Quebec and Newfoundland to Labrador.

Driving the last spike.   *The Public Archives of Canada.*

DATES OF INTEREST

November 1
All Saint's Day. In Quebec, it has long been a French Canadian tradition that after church, the men 'go into the bush' to work in lumbering and logging camps until the spring.

November 4, 1838
Rebels attacked Caughnawaga, near Montreal, while the Indians were at church. Rushing out, the Indians put the rebels to flight.

November 6, 1837
Thomas Storrow Brown led the 'Sons of Liberty' to attack the Doric Club, Montreal. This was the beginning of the Rebellion in Lower Canada. The office of the 'Vindicator', a patriot paper, was wrecked in Montreal.

A popular drink served at dances in the forts of the traders of the North West, about 1800, was shrub, a punch concocted of rum, grated nutmeg, sugar, lemon or orange juice.

On Grosse Island, near Quebec, 'lie the remains of 5,424 persons, who fleeing from pestilence and famine in Ireland, in 1847, found in America, but a grave.'

The Orderly Book of Fort Cumberland (formerly Fort Beauséjour) Nova Scotia, 1759-60, records concern because the soldiers were eating too much molasses which was felt prejudicial to good health. To keep them fit, officers were directed to use the molasses to brew beer.

November takes its name from the Latin word 'novem' or nine, for it used to be the ninth month in the old Roman calendar.

A translation is given here of part of the document to which King William III put his name and seal on Nov. 1, 1697:
'Be it known whereas in the year 1677 certain territories situated in the Northern part of America were discovered and taken possession of in OUR NAME, not previously occupied by anyone, but having become known by shipwrecks which took place on the coasts thereof, under the name of Labrador Corte Real and Estotiland, and that since the taking of the aforesaid possession on the 23rd of September of the year mentioned Our arms of Nassau and Orange were hoisted there to the end that we might be able to dispose thereof to the people who might be disposed to establish any commerce there under Our authority and protection. . . Then We promise him, the aforesaid Joseph de la Penja and his successors, Our protection and support in the possession of the aforesaid lease as Our vassal against any vexations and molestations. Done at Het Loo on the first of November, 1697.
William R.'

DID YOU KNOW THAT

Toronto, 2sd. November, 1857

My dear Galt,

. . . You call yourself a Rouge. There may have been at one time a reddish tinge about you, but I could observe it becoming by degrees fainter. In fact you are like Byron's Dying Dolphin, exhibiting a series of colours – 'the last still loveliest' – and that last is 'true blue', being the colour I affect.

Seriously you would make a decent Conservative, if you gave your own judgment a fair chance and cut loose from Holton and Dorion and those other beggars. So pray do become true blue at once: it is a good standing colour and bears washing.

Yours always,
John A. Macdonald.

In the elections of 1857, Alexander Tilloch Galt announced that he would stand as an independent and denounced the Upper Canada Opposition. He was again returned for Sherbrooke by acclamation.

Long before the farmers began to speak up, James Gay, self-styled 'Master of all Poets and Poet Laureate of Canada' wrote these lines in Guelph, where he lived about 1834.

It's by the plough the farmer thrives,
And keeps poor men happy with their wives:
Through him, too, may well be said,
That little children receive their bread.
In fact we need not frown or brawl,
The honest farmer pays for all.

∽ ∽

The Canadian woodlands are owned largely by the Crown, that is, the people of Canada. About 80% of the productive forests are publicly owned and administered by the ten provincial governments.

∽ ∽

The list of signers to the Requisition to Mr. Galt in favour of annexation, numbers 1213 of the staunch yeomanry of this country. (The Montreal **Pilot** says those holding rank in the service of Her Majesty are being asked to explain their conduct.)

Sherbrooke Gazette, November 10, 1849.

Baked Buffalo and Beer Pie, 19th Century.

Cut in one inch cubes, 4 pounds collops of Buffalo meat, preferably from leg. Season well with salt, pepper and sage. Roll in flour. Brown in heavy pan in very hot oil. Transfer to a braising pot.

Cut up 3 medium sized onions, 3 carrots, 3 stalks celery, and 3 potatoes in half-inch cubes. Toss in the same hot oil, for a few minutes, until they begin to cook. Add to the meat along with the savoury bits in the pan. Take up the oil with 3 tablespoons flour. Let brown in oven.

Heat 2 pints beef stock, or broth made with Buffalo bones. Add to this 2 tablespoons tomato purée and 1 pint beer (preferably stout). Blend into meat slowly and smoothly. Add herb bag of a garlic clove, bay leaf, parsley stems, 3 cloves and pinch of thyme. Simmer until meat is tender. Remove herb bag. Turn the ragout into a colander to separate the sauce. Divide meat and vegetables into pot pie dishes. Cover each with pie-paste, brush with milk. Bake to a golden brown.

About 1893 large posters like the following were posted in railroad stations:

'To Homeseekers in British Columbia. For sale cheap. Town lots in Kilowna. Beautifully situated on the shore of Lake O'Kanagan, near to Lord Aberdeen's fruit farm. Also blocks of 5 to 50 acres each, suitable for fruit and hop culture, and 19,000 acres choice farm lands, in quantities to suit purchasers. Apply to O'Kanagan Land and Colonization Co., Kilowna.'

Sir Alexander Tilloch Galt.
The Public Archives of Canada.

The Indians call November 'The Mad Moon' or 'Akwutinoo'wepesim — 'The Frost Moon'. Around James Bay, the Crees name this month 'Wawaypesim — The Wavy Goose Moon.'

Many were concerned about the choice of a name for our new confederation. Suggestions sent to the Toronto 'Globe', in Nov. 1864 included Tupona, from the first letters of The United Provinces of North America; and British Esfiga, from the first letters of English, Scottish, French, Irish, German and Aboriginal.

∽ ∽

November birthstones are the topaz and the citrine. The topaz is thought to have healing powers and is also the symbol of loyalty and uprightness.

NOVEMBER

If a Nova Scotian says to you 'Drop by for supper, we're having Solomon Gundy,' don't expect to meet an old sea-faring character. What the friend means is that they will be having a time-honoured favourite dish of salt herring, fixed with hot vinegar and served with potatoes in their jackets.

Another half-year of this paper having expired, the printer will be obliged to his customers if they will call and settle for it as the expence of conducting it is very great.

Nova Scotia 'Packet and General Advertiser', Shelburne, N.S., Nov. 23, 1786.

There are amongst the laws of the Eskimos –

1. No man shall do any work requiring the use of tools after sunset. The women may sew, make garments, or chew boots, but no man shall work.

2. No person shall eat walrus and deer meat upon the same day.

3. The carcases of all large animals slain during the winter shall be equally divided amongst all.

4. Any person finding driftwood secures ownership by placing stones upon it.

5. When a seal is harpooned, and gets off with the harpoon, the first harpooner loses all claim to it, when the float becomes detached.

6. If two hunters strike a bird at the same time, it shall be equally divided between them.

7. Whoever is first to see a bear has ownership, no matter who slays it.

8. After slaying a bear, the man who kills it shall hang up his hunting implement, together with the bladder of the beast, in some high conspicuous place, for at least three days, and for four days he shall be separated from his wife.

9. When a walrus is slain, the successful hunter shall be separated from his wife for at least one day.

J. W. Tyrrell 'The Canadian Magazine', 1894.

'This stone was well and truly laid by Lieut. Colonel Edwin A. Baker, OBE, M.C., Croix-de-Guerre, B.Sc., LL.D. on Remembrance Day, November 11th, 1954.'

With his fingers he read the inscription on the cornerstone which he had just tapped into place in the library wing of Bakerwood, the new home of the Canadian National Institute for the Blind. He was thinking of the days ahead for the CNIB, not back forty years, to the day when a sniper's bullet in World War One had blinded him at the age of 21. He may have thought a little of 1918 when the Canadian National Institute for the Blind received its charter. Financier Lewis Miller Wood became its first president, and Col. Baker the Vice-President; and here they were still working together, with all sorts of ideas for using the modern facilities of the new building. The name Bakerwood was taken from their two names.

'Tact is the saving virtue without which no woman can be a success, as a nurse or not. She may have all the others, but without tact she is a failure ... It is one of the greatest of human blessings that so many women are so full of tact. The calamity happens when a woman who has all the other riches of life just lacks that one thing.'

Sir William Osler, address to nurses, 1913.

The memory of the Redman
How can it pass away,
While his names of music linger
On each mount and stream and bay;
While Musquodoboit's waters
Roll sparkling to the main,
While falls the laughing sunbeam
On Chegogin's fields of grain?

Jack Miner, Kingsville, 1930. *The Public Archives of Canada.*

Richard Huntington, Yarmouth, Nova Scotia, about 1875; 'Indian Names of Acadia'.

DID YOU KNOW THAT

'The Jack Miner Bird Sanctuary these November days is one of the wonders of the world ... many thousands of wild fowl, mostly geese, resting and feeding after their long flight from Hudson Bay area. How these birds can wing their unerring way. ... to the fields and ponds which comprise the Sanctuary is beyond the explanation or comprehension of human beings.'
        'Windsor Daily Star,' November 14, 1952.

November eleventh was called Armistice Day until 1931, when the name was changed to Remembrance Day.

On this day those who died in the two world wars are honoured with a ceremony at the National War Memorial, Ottawa, which while attended by high Government officials is arranged by the Royal Canadian Legion. Many other observances are held throughout the Dominion.

The symbolic red poppy made by disabled war veterans is seen from coast to coast, distributed at a tag day organized by the Royal Canadian Legion.

Old Christ Church, built in 1840 at The Pas, Manitoba, has furniture made by carpenters of a party searching for the ill-fated explorer Sir John Franklin. (It was in 1845 that his third expedition sought a North West Passage, and met with disaster.)

'Indians shall, so long as they continue in Friendship, Receive Presents of Blankets, Tobacco, and some Powder and Shot; and promise yearly upon the first of October to come or their Delegates and Receive the said Presents and Renew their Friendship and Submissions.

The Indians shall use their best Endeavours to save the Lives and Goods of any Shipwrecked on this coast, and shall conduct the people Saved to Halifax with their Goods, and a Reward adequate to the Salvadge shall be given them.'

Treaty between Micmac Chief Jean Baptiste Cope and the Government, Halifax, Nov. 22, 1752.

THE NOTMAN STUDIO,
Opposite Parliament Buildings,

The Public Archives of Canada.

OUR GRASS ROOTS

William Notman, the exceptional photographer, was 30 when he arrived in Canada in 1856, and was soon posing nearly every Canadian of note, and many of the international 'greats'.

In November, 1956, his collection of more than 500,000 plates and pictures were presented to the McCord Museum of McGill University by Maclean's Magazine, Empire Universal Films Limited and the Maxwell Cummings Family Foundation.

Notman excelled at the 'composite picture', which meant pasting separate photographs on a large master copy. He once used 1200 subjects in one picture, discarding many more plates than he used.

This imaginative resourceful camera artist was years ahead of his time. His famous outdoor 'Trapping the Carcajou' was made **inside** his studio. Notman used salt for snow and produced a blizzard by blowing a cloud of Chinese white paint through an atomizer onto the varnished side of his negatives. He thought nothing of 'tying people down with cord, or propping them up with books, stools or boxes.'

During the early French-régime, grants of land were made to the 'seigneur', who was obliged to develop the holdings, render homage to the Crown and service to his tenants, or 'censitaires'. This latter term was so little liked that the word 'habitant' was used instead, even in legal documents.

Around Rathwell, Manitoba, about 1890, if you asked a neighbour, 'How are you?', he would likely reply, 'Finer than frog's hair.'

'Presents of money injure both the giver and the receiver, and destroy the equilibrium of friendship, and diminish independence.'
Justice Thomas Chandler Haliburton, about 1840.

DATES OF INTEREST

November 12, 1757
Belêtre, with 300 Canadians and Indians, surprised a German settlement, at the German Flats, on the Mohawk, killed 50, made the rest prisoners and burned the place.

November 12, 1880
An explosion in the 'Foord' pit, at Stellarton, Nova Scotia, killed 50 miners.

November 14, 1606
When Champlain and Poutrincourt returned to Port Royal after a map-making exploration as far as Nantucket Island, they were greeted by the first play ever presented in Canada, 'The Theatre of Neptune'. The poet, Marc Lescarbot, had arranged a tableau showing Neptune in a floating chariot, drawn by six Tritons.

November 14, 1775
Benedict Arnold attacked the Gate of St. Louis, Quebec City, but was speedily repulsed.

November 15, 1690
Three supply ships arrived at Quebec, having evaded Sir William Phips, who had taken Port Royal, and was attempting to capture Quebec.

November 1840
A magnetical and metereological observatory established at Toronto by the Imperial Government.

November 15, 1827
Postage on a letter from Quebec to Sherbrooke, 9d. or 15 cents.

Michaelmas Day, Nov. 11, was devoted to business in French Canada. Each 'habitant' came forward to pay his rent to the Seigneur plus a small fee for the use of the grist mill and bake oven.

OLD TIMOTHY

'In the Nor'west folks say the gold an' silver mines'll peter out, but the tourists'll keep a-comin!'

Here Lies
General Bain
Who Died in his Bist
Clothes, A Rispictable
Man — A Rayl Ould
Irish Protestant.

The legend on a small wooden slab, at the grave of the General (self-styled) of Sandy Beach, in Ontario, about 1890.

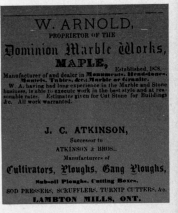

Wonderful strawberries grow at Inuvik, 127 miles north of the Arctic Circle. Twenty-four hours of daylight during the summer months offer record growth facilities. The berries winter just under the snow-covered brush. Vegetables do well, with cabbages that weigh 25 lbs. or more. Altogether, excellent results reward those who have experimented with other fruits and vegetables.

Polar bear makes delicious steaks. Remove excess fat or meat will taste too sweet, broil over hot fire, or boil in pot with onions. Or grind into bearburgers or simply cut into thin steaks to be partly frozen, until they do not bend to touch.

The first Canadian Bank Note was issued by the Canada Bank in 1792 for 'five chelins.'

Deportment in New France (1685-1686):

'The vivacity of their daughter necessitates a few diversions ... one may deign to permit a few honest dances with her own sex only and in the presence of her mother, and never in the presence of men for this mixing of sexes is the cause of the inconveniences and disorders of balls.'

It was in 1922 that our five cent pieces were increased in size, and no longer made of silver, but of nickel, tombac and steel. (Tombac is 88% copper, 12% zinc.)

Two years before, in 1920, the one cent pieces, of bronze, were reduced in size. In that year the Mint issued 6,901,626 large ones and 15,472,153 small ones.

Louis Joseph Papineau.   The Public Archives of Canada.

Catmint tea was used by western homesteaders for stomach sickness, but in the Maritimes it was thought to make a 'peaceful man very fierce'. Pennyroyal was prescribed for internal injuries, for sore eyes, and to cleanse and purify water. Another opinion has it that pennyroyal should be avoided as it makes a person see double.

Madder to stop toothache, a large ivy blade called 'Adam and Eve' to heal cuts and burns, and a liverwort plant, 'trippe de roche', to cure liver ailments were universally recommended.

Others cured fever, bilious headache, ulcers, clergyman's sore throat, falling hair and worms. For the linen closet, there were sweet woodruff, rosemary, lavender and sweet violet; and for the kitchen sage, spearmint, thyme, tarragon, marjoram, sweet basil and dill.

Always delicate, Laurier was well past middle life before any insurance company would risk a policy on his life, yet he lived to 78. On his 76th birthday, Nov. 20, 1917, he wrote to Archbishop Bruchesi: 'Accept my sincere thanks for your good wishes. The years have brought nothing good. I owe only gratitude to Providence for the health I enjoy ... and after all health is the greatest good of life.'

DATES OF INTEREST

November 16, 1686
Denonville, governor of New France, wrote to France, 'I have a mind to go straight to Albany, storm their fort, and burn everything.'

November 16, 1837
Warrants issued for the arrest of Louis Joseph Papineau, patriote leader.

November 17, 1865
Fifteen citizens volunteered to spring the trap for criminal Stanislas Barreau, found guilty of murdering a girl and woman at Laprairie, Quebec, that ancient settlement of 1667. The public hangman, however, officiated at the Montreal Jail.

November 17, 1866
British Columbia and Vancouver were united.

Canadian-born William Hall was the first Negro, the first Nova Scotian and the first Canadian sailor to win the Victoria Cross.

Volunteering for service at the relief of Lucknow, Nov. 16, 1857, he showed remarkable courage. He was the son of a Virginia slave, who was brought to Halifax in the War of 1812.

The purple fireweed (Epilobium Angustifolium) was chosen as the official floral emblem for the Yukon Territory on Nov. 16, 1957.

OLD TIMOTHY

'Provin' up wuz what every homesteader aimed to do. Jist to meet every regulation an' make the quarter section his'n.'

'Charity is infinitely divisible. He who has a little can always give a little.'

Peter McArthur, 'To Be Taken With Salt', 1903.

In the days when the Arctic was much more remote than it is today, the hospitable Eskimos would share their meals with explorers, who were among the few that ventured far North. Delicacies like raw blubber or a seal's flipper were often sent as a present from another seal-hunter living near the snowhouse of the host. Boiled seal meat would be followed by blood-soup, made by adding cold seal-blood to the broth in which the meat had been cooked.

'Industry, Intelligence and Integrity' was the motto of Toronto adopted by the first mayor, William Lyon Mackenzie, in 1835.

An explorer of Lake Superior in 1844 wrote that he looked forward to the luxury of beaver tails for breakfast, as nothing else was as good. He added that a beaver tail of about nine inches weighed nearly a pound and was almost enough for a man's breakfast.

'If a Frenchman has a fiddle, he doesn't need sleep.'
Quebec saying.

Remedy for Sea-Sickness

Take as much Cayenne pepper as you can rightly bear, in a basin of hot soup, and, it is said, all sickness, nausea, and squeamishness will disappear. *1750*

Riel addressing the Jury in the Court House, Regina. 1885.   *The Public Archives of Canada.*

DID YOU KNOW THAT

Many travellers have been impressed by the 'Statue of the Virgin' on Cape Trinity when they sail up the Saguenay River, but few know that it was unveiled in 1881 as a thanksgiving offering by a man who recovered from a serious illness on that voyage, passing the cliffs.

The 25 foot statue weighs 5 tons and is 600 feet above the water. It is the work of artist Louis Jobin, who was born in Quebec in 1845, and whose wood carvings adorn many churches and shrines in the province. He made this 'Statue of the Virgin' of rough-hewn pieces of wood covered by lead sheets.

In recent years as some boats approach the shrine, the captain turns the spotlight on the statue, while the **Ave Maria** is heard over the loudspeakers.

Le Canadien, the first French newspaper in Quebec City, on Nov. 22, 1806, styled the British 'strangers and intruders'. The **Quebec Mercury** however said 'This province is far too French for a British colony. It is absolutely necessary that we exert all our efforts, to oppose the increase of the French and the augmentation of their influence. After 47 years possession, it is now fitting that the Province become truly British.'

OUR GRASS ROOTS

When Louis Riel was executed by hanging in the Mounted Police barracks at Regina on November 16, 1885, he said to his priest confessor, 'I swear as I am about to appear before God that the shooting of Thomas Scott was not a crime. It was a political necessity. . . . I commanded the shooting, believing it necessary to save the lives of hundreds of others.' To a guard, who asked for a souvenir, Riel said, 'I have nothing but my heart, and I gave it long ago to my country.'

Sir George Head, a brother of Sir Francis Bond Head, described an 1814 winter social assembly for cards and dancing in Fredericton, N.B. in 'Forest Scenes and Incidents in the Wilds of North America'. He wrote of his discomfiture as the ladies dressed for departure, 'All the snowboots required fastening, and to fasten them it was indispensable to stoop. Some ladies had chairs, but most had not; so that the variety of attitudes in which the female figure on that occasion was displayed, I shall not readily forget.'

NOVEMBER

DATES OF INTEREST

November 24, 1648
Barbe Meusnier was the first white child born at Montreal.

November 24, 1648
A thousand Mohawks and Senecas took the warpath for the Hurons.

November 24, 1807
Joseph Brant, principal chief of the Six Nations Indians, died. He had translated part of the Church of England prayer book into Mohawk.

November 24, 1869
Louis Riel, 'President of the Provisional Government in Red River'' took Fort Garry, and its contents.

November 25, 1743
An ordinance restrained religious communities from acquiring more land without royal permission.

November 27, 1877
The Halifax Fishery Commission concluded that the United States pay $5,500,000 for fishing privileges for twelve years. This was paid up the following year.

OLD TIMOTHY

'When folks walk, they see things; when they drive, they don't see much; and when they fly, they see nothin.'

Cure for Arctic fever – Put man on ice.

'Time is like a woman and pigs; the more you want it to go — the more it won't.'
Justice Thomas Chandler Haliburton, about 1840.

Montreal's first street car, a magnificent model of white and gold paint, took passengers in 1892. It was called 'The Rocket'.

La Tire (or taffy, or molasses kisses), is traditionally eaten in French Canada on Nov. 25, the feast day of Saint Catherine, the patron saint of unmarried girls of a 'certain age.'

The smaller Eskimo carvings, sometimes called 'mitt pieces,' are carried in the Eskimo's mitt to show to neighbours or friends, or to work on in the odd moments of waiting while on a hunting or fishing trip. They might serve as a lucky talisman to ensure success, or as a record of some incident.

Do you know that there is a Punkey-doodle Corner in Southwestern Ontario, a hamlet called Ecum Secum in Nova Scotia, and The Little Waterhen River in Manitoba? Other highly descriptive names include Driedmeat Hill (where the Indians did just that); Justice, a small village near Brandon, Man. (which we hope lives up to its name); Scratching River and Fatigue Mountain, in the West; and puzzlers in Newfoundland, such as Goobies, Witless Bay and Seldom-Come-Bay.

It is, I believe, not an uncommon mode with Americans when they talk to amuse rather than convince.
Justice Thomas Chandler Haliburton, about 1840.

When Louis de Buade, Comte de Pallau et de Frontenac, died at 78 on Nov. 28, 1698, his critics, and there were many, wrote a commentary on the funeral oration, which is still preserved in Quebec. The orator's remarks about his fidelity to friends were contradicted with 'What friends? Was it persons of the other sex? Of these he was always fond, and too much for the honour of some.'

He provided that masses be said for his widow after her death, left her his small property, and requested that his heart be sent her in a small silver case. The story goes that she refused this token, saying, 'I never had his heart while he was living. I do not want it now that he is dead.'

Scottish Immigrants at Quebec City. The Public Archives of Canada.

DID YOU KNOW THAT

Two million Scots in Canada observe the anniversary of Scotland's patron saint on Nov. 30, with the cutting of the haggis, and the dancing of reels to the music of bagpipes. Grand balls in Montreal, Toronto, Winnipeg, Vancouver and Quebec feature the Cross of St. Andrew, the Lion Rampant and the French Crest, depicting the Auld Alliance between the Scots and the French.

Some authorities hold that 'haggis' is from the French 'hachis' which means minced or hash. For haggis, itself, is oatmeal mixed with grated sheep's heart, liver and lights, suet, onions and seasoning, all boiled in a sheep's stomach – served with a dram of whiskey.

'It (Ontario) will be the very mockery of a province, 300 or 400 families scattered over a country some 400 miles in length, not having any towns and scarcely a village in the province.'
Adam Lymburner, 1791.

'The Iroquois was the Indian of Indians. A thorough savage, yet a finished and developed savage, he is perhaps an example of the highest elevation which man can reach without emerging from his primitive condition of the hunter.'

Francis Parkman, the historian.

*He has not the courage of a mouse, nor has he the sense of right and desire for the people's good ... He is a jobber at heart; the benefit of the people is his last thought in considering a public question.'

The Toronto 'Globe' about Sir Alexander Tilloch Galt (1817-1893).

The idea is the same but the French express it differently.

We take 'French leave' but the French take 'Congé à l'anglaise' (English leave).

'Poor as a church mouse' goes Biblical to become 'Pauvre comme Job' (poor as Job).

In cold weather, we get 'Goose Flesh' but our French friends suffer from 'chaire de poule' (chicken flesh).

When the genial host is pouring drinks, you might say 'Pour me just a drop'. But your French brother would remark, if you can imagine such a thing, 'Pour moi, deux fois rien' or 'Give me twice nothing.'

'Doing things the round – about way' becomes 'Chercher midi a quatorze heures (looking for noon at two o'clock)'.

'Like two peas in a pod' becomes 'Se ressemblent comme deux gouttes d'eau (like two drops of water)'.

We say a thing sells 'like hot cakes' but our neighbours put it this way – 'Ca se vend comme des pains chauds (sells like hot breads)'.

An advertisement in the 'Quebec Herald' and 'Universal Miscellany' for November 24, 1788, reads:
'For Sale – by Fr. Glackemeyer. Two excellent new PianoForte's, with a neat leather cover warranted to be of the best tone, and to stand tune a long time. The following Harpsicord music, Niccolais Sonatas, Opers 3 and 7; Overture by Jomelly, do to the Opera Rosina. A choice collection of songs neatly bound, Operas, the Padlock, Poor Soldier and Grettna Green. A collection of Divine Music. Two volumes of Military Music fit for bands, compleat by several Masters. 2 Volume do. Flack's Divertimento's Compleat. Bassoon and Hautboy Reeds. Fiddle pegs and Bridges. The Best Harpsicord, Piano Forte and Guitar Strings, The best Roman Fiddle Strings. A collection of Country Dances and Minuets for the years 1787, 1788 with their proper figures. Tuening hammers and Pitch Forks. Harpsicords, Piano Fortes, Guitars repaired and tuned on the shortest notice and most reasonable terms.'

St. Andrew's Ball.
Ball dresses from fifteen shillings upwards. C. Healy, laceman, 219 Notre Dame Street, Montreal.

Advt. 'New Era', Montreal, Nov. 1857.

The North British Society, Halifax, will celebrate the anniversary of their tutelar Saint by dining in the Masonic Hall on the 30th. All members, Scotchmen and their descendants, are invited to leave their names with the secretary. President, Andrew D. Russel.

Weekly Chronicle, Halifax, November, 1822.

The fur of royalty sounds better when one calls it ermine, but actually it is the coat of the stoat, a small animal closely related to the weasel. Synonymous with elegance and luxury, this pure white creature with the black-tipped tail is found around Hudson's Bay.

Sir James Douglas, governor of Vancouver Island in 1851, was almost despotic, yet wise and conscientious. Tanned from his life as a Hudson Bay chief trader, he was big and commanding, and 'walked out' in Victoria, daily, followed by a retinue of servants, in uniform. Church attendance was compulsory for all at his court.

Sir James Douglas. From Canada and its Provinces. Shortt and Doughty. Toronto, 1914. The Public Archives of Canada.

OUR GRASS ROOTS

In the lobby of the Legislative Chamber is a tablet bearing the following inscription:
SIR JAMES DOUGLAS, K.C.B.
1803-1877
'FATHER OF BRITISH COLUMBIA'
Fur trader and statesman. In his early life he was associated first with the North West Company and later with the Hudson's Bay Company. He founded Fort Victoria in 1843. By his firm and wise rule as Governor of Vancouver Island, 1851-1864, and Governor of British Columbia, 1858-1864, he laid the foundations of this Province.

'Good God, what sums the nursing of that ill-throven, hardvisaged, and ill-favoured brat, Nova Scotia, has cost to this wittol* nation.'

Edmund Burke, in the House of Commons, Great Britain, 1780.
* *'Wittol' means cuckolded and submissive.*

DECEMBER

The man who invented the game of basketball, in 1891, Dr. James A. Naismith, said 'No team like this has been seen on any basketball floor anywhere!' High praise, but not too high. In the quarter century from 1915 to 1940, the girls of the Edmonton Grads Basketball Team lost only 20 of the 522 games they played. They won against other Canadians, against Americans, and against Europeans. The won all 27 of the 27 games they played at the Olympic Games in Paris, Amsterdam, Los Angeles and Berlin, scoring 1,863 points. Their opponents made less than 300 points.

From 'the backwoods of Manitoba,' at the end of the 1800's, came many verses from Isaac White, the rhyming crusader. Here is one on vaccination:

Vile toxin is a blighting curse,
Compulsion makes pure vaccine worse.

Dec. 1, 1869 'The Red River Pioneer' Winnipeg, first and only issue which was sold to the 'New Nation,' Winnipeg. The four page issue combined the two papers.
'The Morning Leader', Dec. 1, 1905.

"A View of Three Rivers, from the road leading to Pointe du Lac" by J. Peachey.   The Public Archives of Canada.

DID YOU KNOW THAT

'Cash only.' 'One price plainly marked.' 'Goods satisfactory, or money refunded.' 'A square deal for everyone.'

These business principles, taken for granted today, were considered revolutionary when Timothy Eaton opened his small drygoods store at Yonge and Queen Streets, Toronto on Dec. 8, 1869, two years after Confederation. Hard cash had seldom appeared at a sale. People had bartered a bag of wheat for a piece of cloth, and so on. The store, 24 feet by 60 feet, was staffed by two men, a woman and a boy.

The great 'Bourdon' or tower bell of Notre Dame Cathedral, Montreal, weighs 14½ tons, one ton more than Big Ben, of Westminster Cathedral, London.

When scarcely nineteen, John Strachan, who was to become the first Bishop of Toronto, was being examined for the post of a parish school at Kettle, Scotland, which was worth £50 per annum. The examiner remarked that he 'was not great things, but would be the best there notwithstanding'.

When Samuel de Champlain came to Canada at the beginning of the 17th century, he was accompanied by mining engineers who reported copper mineralization in the Bay of Chaleur area and 'silver occurrence' in St. Mary's Bay, Nova Scotia. But it was not until about the 1730's that first commercial use was made of Canadian ores. French settlers then began to use iron deposits around Three Rivers, Que. The metal was used for pots and pans, ploughshares and cannon balls.

'Don't work all your life to make a living but work to live all your life.'
Jack Miner, O.B.E.

Incorporated in 1877 when Winnipeg was still a pioneer town, the University of Manitoba is the oldest university in Western Canada.

'Love goes where it is sent'.
Nova Scotia Proverb.

In 1804, just 12 years after Capt. Vancouver came to this coast, William Sturgis, a seafaring merchant from Boston, arrived with 5000 ermine skins from Leipzig. These he sold to the Kimgarnee Indians who prized them for ceremonial purposes. Valuing his ermine at 30 cents each, Capt. Sturgis bartered them at 'five for one sea-otter skin'. These he sold at Canton, China for $50 each.

The hungry settlers relished supporne, a porridge made with corn flour that was boiled a good long time in water, and then eaten with milk. Supporne-cake, fried in slices and served with maple syrup, was considered a great treat.

It is said that there was a sting to the style but no spite in the nature of the distinguished but controversial Bishop Strachan. He himself boasted of 'very good nerves' and said that he could be silent while criticism rolled off him, disturbing neither his meals nor rest. His pockets always gave up a bright sixpence for the small boys who were not frightened as he approached with his threatening walking-stick, invariably whistling a Scottish tune, something he was known to do even in church.

Dr. John Strachan.   The Public Archives of Canada.

OUR GRASS ROOTS

Many stories are told of Dr. John Strachan, the 'Fighting Bishop'. When a member of the Lower House, of U.C., was pondering the legality of expelling Barnabas Bidwell, reformer, author and teacher, in 1821, Dr. Strachan shouted, 'Toorn him oot! Toorn him oot! Never mind the law!'

Another tells how this 'Defender of the Clergy Reserves' ran an advertisement in 1818 in York announcing that the fees for his lectures on Natural Philosophy (the term then applied to Science) would go for painting the 'Blue School.'

The blue-purple violet (Viola palmata, var. Cucullata) was officially introduced as the floral emblem of New Brunswick on Dec. 1, 1936 after considerable activity by the Lieutenant-Governor, Col. Murray MacLaren, the Women's Institutes and the school children.

There is red snow in the Arctic. 'I found it was caused by the juice of a berry which grows on a ground vine at the head of the timber limit, which when pressed gives out a purple juice. ... This juice is absorbed by the Indian's moccasins as he tramps on the berries, and stains the snow as he travels. This by the heat of the sun and the action of gravity on the hillside, is distributed over a wide area, compared with the track, and is visible after all sign of the track is gone.'

'Down the Yukon' William Ogilvie, D.L.S., F.R.G.S., 'Canadian Magazine', 1893.

DATES OF INTEREST

December 1680
The 'Great Comet' appeared, and was visible to the end of Feb. 1681. 'No comet has threatened the earth with a nearer approach.'

December 1, 1775
Gen. Montgomery and Col. Arnold met at Point aux Trembles, near Montreal, before their assault on Quebec.

December 1, 1841
The first copyright was granted for the 'Canadian Spelling Book' by Alex. Davidson, of the Niagara district. It was published by Henry Roswell, Toronto.

December 3, 1804
Found one-half of a fat hog on Humber Plains, Toronto. Supposed fraudulently killed and other half taken away. Finder has dressed the part found, requests owner to pay expenses and take it. (Notice).

December 7, 1837
Sir Francis Head and Col. McNab, with 500 militia, marched from Toronto to Montgomery's Tavern, Yonge Street. They routed 800 rebels and burned the tavern. William Lyon Mackenzie took to flight.

December 7, 1869
Louis Riel made Dr. John Christian Schultz, (later Lieutenant-Governor of Manitoba) a prisoner. He was sentenced to death but escaped.

December 8, 1812
Gen. Porter and Gen. Smyth fought a duel on Grand Island; but as their seconds had carefully drawn the balls from their pistols, both survived.

'She hadn't no ear for music, but she had a capital eye for dirt, and for poor folks that's much better.'

'The Clockmaker, or The Sayings and Doings of Samuel Slick, of Slickville' by Justice Thomas Chandler Haliburton, 1836.

OLD TIMOTHY

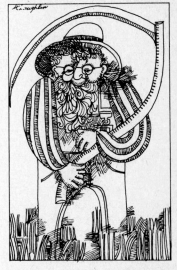

'First year on the homestead an' new-comers knew the ole-timers weren't jokin' when they sed western weather wuz ten months winter an' two months poor sleighin'.'

December birthstones are the turquoise, which promises success in love and money; and the zircon, known in medieval times as a cure for the plague and other ills, especially insomnia.

'The Long Night Moon' is what the Indians call December. They have another name 'Yeyekwu'tinoowepesim' or 'Rimey Moon.'

What strokes came my way at school were not stolen.

The country curé is described as 'Good sense and good humour bundled in six ells of black cloth'.

A child, trained not to answer all prying questions, is told, '. . . not to be a basket full of holes.'

Of a bold person, it is said, 'He was not at home when Shyness called.'

'Other Days, Other Ways', by Georges Bouchard, M.P.

Do you have trouble finding a shiny silver dollar? They were first issued in 1935 for the Silver Jubilee of George V, when 428,120 were minted. By 1962, the number had grown to 1,894,092.

In order that occupants might not overlook convent grounds, building on lands sold by religious orders in 1725 was restricted to one-storey construction. Houses facing the street were allowed no side windows.

A royal proclamation of 1763 giving Eskimos and Indians hunting rights was upheld 200 years later by a Territorial Court Judge who ruled that Matthew Coonungnak, an Eskimo, was not liable to a fine of $200 for shooting a muskox, an animal otherwise protected by law.

Yorkshire folk, who pioneered in Cumberland County, Nova Scotia, relished furmity pudding, of new wheat boiled in milk, for Christmas Eve supper.

December 1758
When Montcalm received a decoration from the King of France, the Indians said 'We neither love nor esteem you the more for it; we love the man and not what hangs upon him.'

'A shining plow makes a full mow.'

Saying of pioneer Ontario farmers.

The flower for December is the narcissus, denoting vanity.

*Louis Joseph Marquis de Montcalm.
The Public Archives of Canada.*

OLD TIMOTHY

'Could'nt fool an Injun about fire-water. Ef it blazed up over the fire, they knew it was good brandy. Ef it put out the fire, they knew water had been added.'

'I find that Newfoundland is said to be celebrated for its codfish, its dogs, its hogs, its fogs and its bogs. That is a very erroneous opinion, I assure you.'

Sir William Whiteway, London, 1897.

DATES OF INTEREST

December 9, 1851
The Young Men's Christian Association was established in Montreal, the first in America.

December 10, 1880
At midnight, the contract for building the C.P.R. was laid before the House.

December 11, 1813
Gen. McClure, at Fort George, fearing the approach of the British, burnt Newark and crossed to Fort Niagara. He burned 149 houses, compelling 400 women and children to seek shelter in the woods in extreme cold.

December 12, 1650
Louis Maheu was born in Quebec and became the first native-born Canadian to practise medicine. In his spare time he was the Quebec harbour master.

December 1792
A bill to abolish slavery failed to pass in Lower Canada. But on July 9th of the next year, the importation of slaves was prohibited. In 1804, there were 142 slaves in the district of Montreal, and more than twice that many in the Province of Quebec.

DID YOU KNOW THAT

'The fisheries of Newfoundland are inexhaustible and are of more value to the Empire than all the silver mines of Peru.'
Lord Bacon, about 1608.

With accommodation for eight patients, the first hospital in Canada, St. Jean de Dieu, at Port Royal, was established in 1629 by the French authorities.
    The Sisters of the Hôpitalières of St. John were able to take care of one hundred patients at the second Canadian hospital at Louisbourg, N.S., which opened in 1724. Running hot and cold water was introduced. Every vessel in the port gave ten pounds of codfish daily as a hospital tax.

'Nothing in the world is more cruel than an Iroquois war. Then the habitant trembles as he eats; no one who leaves the house may count on returning; his sowings and reapings are abandoned for the most part. The seigneur sees all **his lands** pillaged and burnt, nor can he reckon himself safe in his stronghold. The traveller moves but by night. Let anyone work in the fields, either he is massacred or he is suddenly carried off to be burnt alive, or he is felled by a crushing blow to be scalped. Whoever travels up the river by canoe is espied afar off and despite all precautions is tracked through the forests.'
Claude Charles Le Roy de la Potherie, author and soldier, seventeenth century.

A warm Christmas, a cold Easter. (New Brunswick saying.)

The pioneer Acadians of Nova Scotia looked forward to the special réveillon served on their return from midnight mass at Christmas. Awaiting them was a 'Garteau', baked in the household's longest pan, of birds, rabbits, and pork under a rich pastry cover.

THE GREAT FISHERIES OF NEWFOUNDLAND.

Fishing on the Coast of Newfoundland.

Our past records have shown many fathers and sons sharing the same interests, dating back to the adventurous John Cabot who was accompanied by his son Sebastian when he made his fortunate landfall at Newfoundland in 1497. The son afterwards reported that the codfish were so thick off the banks of Newfoundland 'they sumtymes stayed his shippes.'

Ill-fated Henry Hudson and his son John were cast adrift in an open boat by a mutinous crew in the Hudson Bay area in 1611.

Lawrence Ermatinger and his son Charles Oakes Ermatinger were both furtraders in the late 1700's.

Pierre Stanislas Bédard, born in 1762, was a judge and politician in Charlesbourg, Quebec and was followed in both callings by his son Elzéar Bédard.

John Galt, the novelist, of Canada Company fame in 1824, had two sons who followed him in public service — Sir Thomas Galt, Chief Justice of the Ontario Court of Common Pleas, and Sir Alexander Tilloch Galt, who was Canadian High Commissioner in London.

Hon. Justice Thomas Chandler Haliburton, humourist and historian born in Nova Scotia in 1796, had two sons of similar gifts — Sir Arthur Lawrence Haliburton and writer and lawyer Robert Grant Haliburton.

Napoléon Bourassa, architect and writer, born in L'Acadie, L.C., in 1827 had a son Joseph Napoleon Henri Bourassa, journalist and nationalist leader.

Good Husbandry.

Before spring, the farmer attends to whatever can be done NOW, to prevent interrupting the busy season. Wood should be drawn and corded; rails split, corn selected and tools repaired. A deficiency of tools may be now conveniently supplied. Care should be taken to get the BEST tools, even if this should cost a little more. A man can do one-third more work with a good tool, and he will soon pay the additional expense.

From an 1847 Almanac.

OUR GRASS ROOTS

In 1734 post houses for travellers were located every nine miles on the road between Montreal and Quebec. Public conveyances were available at scheduled rates.

Lord Aberdeen, our Governor-General from 1893-1898, came to Canada, not as a stranger. His grandfather concluded the Treaty of Oregon in 1846, fixing the 49th degree of latitude as the boundary line between Canada and the United States, thus securing for Canada the British Columbia Coast. It is said that he fixed this line so that the salmon would not take the fly south of the forty-ninth parallel.

Sir George Simpson, an illegitimate son, who became Governor-in-Chief of Rupert's Land in 1821, had plenty of showmanship. His arrival at a trading post was something to see, for his picked Iroquois Indians responded to his sense of drama.

Just before reaching his destination, he allowed a brief rest and the Indians donned their most ornate feathers. Then with the redskins chanting, the bagpipes skirling and Sir George smiling in elaborate clothes and a high silk hat, the canoes approached like lightning, as the guns at the fort fired in salute.

An impatient man of great energy, Sir George travelled in light express canoes with two secretaries kept at work. Large freight canoes followed with items to barter for rich pelts. He once went from Hudson Bay to the Pacific in 90 days.

How Sir George Simpson came by his piper is a story in itself. A few years after he came to the North West to direct the activities of the Hudson's Bay Company, he wrote the London office to send him a piper. Apparently this did not seem an unusual request, and in 1827, Highlander Colin Fraser appeared to pipe the Governor-in-Chief with all formal ceremony to the dining hall. The piper accompanied Simpson on all his canoe trips, and his music came to be known on all the waterways.

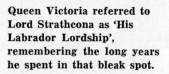
The red wild rose (Rosa Acicularis) is the floral emblem of Alberta. A suggestion, by an Edmonton newspaper editor, interested the Women's Institutes and the Dept. of Education, who had the school children make the choice in the early 1930's.

> *Rudyard Kipling wrote these lines on Halifax:*
> *'Into the mists, my guardian prows put forth,*
> *Behind the mists my virgin ramparts lie,*
> *The Warden of the Honour of the North,*
> *Sleepless and veiled am I .'*

> *Farmers! Beware!*
> *The enemies of the King and the People, – of the Constitution,*
> *and*
> *Sir Francis Head,*
> *Are, day and night, spreading*
> *LIES*
> *They say Sir Francis Head is recalled, – Sir Francis Head is NOT recalled, but is supported by the King and His Ministers.*
> *They say TITHES are to be claimed in Upper Canada. – TITHES shall NOT be claimed in Upper Canada says a permanent Act of Parliament.*
> *FARMERS*
> *Believe not a word these AGITATORS say, but think for yourselves, and SUPPORT SIR FRANCIS HEAD, the friend of . . .*

Part of a broadside used in the election of 1836, Upper Canada.

• • • • • • • •

Gold was discovered on the porcupine-shaped island in the Cockrane district of Northern Ontario early in the 1900's.

The story of Porcupine, or Golden City, which developed into the great gold-mining area of the Western Hemisphere, is bright with names like Gold Island, the Golden Stairway and the Dome Mine.

Overcoming incredible hardships, prospectors George Bannerman and Tom Geddes staked the first claims, squaring a small spruce on which they marked 'G. B. and T. G., July 13, 1909.'

Do not comb your spinach. Just muss it up. Negligee appearance is essential. If two stalks lie parallel it is not fit to eat. After the spinach has been towsled and chucked about a good bit, sift two handfuls of coarse sand over it and place on the stove to boil. Of course, stick in some water first. But don't forget the sand. Spinach without sand in it would not only be improper but illegal. Serve hot.

Bob (Chambers) Edwards, 'Calgary Eye-Opener'.

'The changes in the bill of fare are rather curious as one goes through the country. At Athabasca moose and buffaloe, here rabbits and reindeer tongues, hereafter on Peace River, probably Bearmeat on which they largely depend, then, on the plains exclusively Buffaloe. Sometimes a Beaver here . . . very good. I suppose you know that in Lower Canada, the Beaver is allowed to be 'Maigre' and fetches a great price in Lent . . . The tail is the great delicacy with the moose on the contrary it's the nose.' Fort Simpson, McKenzie's River, 1844.

'In Search of the Magnetic Pole' by John Henry Lefroy, a soldier-surveyor.

'I would not wish to say anything disparaging about the capital, but it is hard to say anything good about it. Ottawa is not a handsome city and does not appear to be destined to become one either.'
Sir Wilfrid Laurier, 1884.

'It's no use to make fences unless the land is cultivated.'
Justice Thomas Chandler Haliburton, about 1840.

Queen Victoria referred to Lord Strathcona as 'His Labrador Lordship', remembering the long years he spent in that bleak spot.

Montreal had its first electric light in 1878, from a power plant at Dowd Street, between Bleury and St. Alexander Sts. Within five years, it was taken over by the Royal Electric Company.

Lord Strathcona and Mount Royal. The Public Archives of Canada.

OUR GRASS ROOTS

Canada has long been famous for the manufacture of 'snuff'. From the time a Canadian 'habitant' awakens in the morning, till he goes to bed at night, the tobacco pipe is seldom out of his mouth. The men smoke so much that they have not time to take snuff; but the snuffmaker is amply compensated by 'the ladies', who, of all ranks and of all ages, are greatly addicted to 'snuff taking', and a filthy custom it is. It most assuredly assists their stoves and dry winter atmosphere, in giving them a withered appearance, and premature marks of age.'

'Letters From Canada', London, England, 1809.

The Artist, Paul Kane, who travelled thousands of miles by canoe, horseback and snowshoe, describes Christmas 1848 at the Big House of the Hudson's Bay Company Chief Factor Rowand at Fort Edmonton. The most palatial building between Norway House and the Pacific Ocean, it was called 'Rowand's Folly.' Kane wrote 'No table cloth shed its snowy whiteness over the board, no silver candelabra interfered with the simple magnificence. Bright tin plates and dishes reflected the jolly faces of Indians, voyageurs, half-breeds and burnished gold can give no truer zest to a feast.'

A cure-all trusted by the Indians of the N.W.T. was a mixture of lard and turpentine, which they ate, drank or rubbed on, depending on the ailment.

For snow blindness they placed wet tea leaves over the eyes, a remedy that the pioneers used also.

White settlers and Indians, alike, tried to prevent dread diptheria by inhaling fumes of sulphur that had been sprinkled over hot coals or rocks.

Parsley, infused with boiling water, made a soothing liquid for tired or inflamed eyes.

Old time remedies.

Domestic Champagne

60	*gallons*	*cider*
3	„	*clear spirits*
2½	„	*honey*

Boil and ferment.

'Household Receipts by a Montreal Lady', 1867.

Our wood paying subscribers will please send us a few cords of wood at their earliest convenience. 'Cornwall Observer', December 18, 1835.

In the late 1700's in Halifax, hostesses were preparing orgeat, a syrup of barley water and capillaire, a syrup of maiden hair fern, which they flavoured with orange flower water and served at the Christmas assemblies for cards and dancing.

OLD TIMOTHY

'Things move so doggone fast in the Northland that a feller is an old pioneer in Frobisher Bay in jist ten years.'

North Aspect of Halifax, 1781, by E. Hicks. *The Public Archives of Canada*

DID YOU KNOW THAT

'I was obliged to take two kegs of alcohol, overruled by my partners (Messrs. Dond McTavish and Jo McDonald Gart) for I had made it a law to myself, that no alcohol should pass the Mountains in my company, and thus be clear of the sad sight of drunkenness, and its many evils; but these gentlemen insisted upon alcohol being the most profitable article that could be taken to the Indian trade. In this I knew that they had miscalculated; accordingly when we came to the defiles of the Mountains I placed the two Kegs of Alcohol on a vicious horse; and by noon the Kegs were empty, and in pieces, the Horse rubbing his load against the Rocks to get rid of it; I wrote my partners what I had done; and that I would do the same to every Keg of Alcohol and for the next six years I had charge of the fur trade on the west side of the Mountains. No further attempt was made to introduce spiritous liquors.'

David Thompson in his journal, 1807.

The first lighthouse in Canada was built by the French at Louisbourg, Nova Scotia, in 1733, as a stone tower, 66 feet high, with a blazing circle of oil-fed wicks to provide the light. In 1738, a lighthouse was built on Sambro Island marking the entrance to Halifax Harbour. In 1788 another was erected at Cape Roseway to serve Shelburne harbour. Saint John, N.B., acquired its first lighthouse on Partridge Island in 1791.

Xmas Plum Pudding.

Take one quart of brandy, two handfuls of plums and raisins, a chunk of suet, some salt and a lot of flour. Knead the last three ingredients together, pouring into yourself sufficient brandy to keep from getting tired. When to sufficient consistency, hang it on the clothesline and hit smartly with a yule log. Roll into a round ball, try and raise it slowly over your head with one hand to see if it is heavy enough and then saturate plentifully with brandy. Set fire to the mess and serve quickly. Return to the kitchen and put balance of brandy out of pain.

Bob (Chambers) Edwards.

People do all sorts of things to choose a name. Almost like a business partnership, Kenora, Ont. is a combination of the first two letters of Keewatin, Norman and Rat Portage.

Something of the same method produced Estevan, which is taken from the names of George Stephen (Lord Mount Stephen) and Sir William Van Horne, the Canadian Pacific Railway moguls.

'And so the old year has beautifully passed. What a wonderful record it has left in science, in research . . . The human unit and the composite of races and nations are seething with unrest, change, and re-formations. Upheaval first; what price results?' *Diary of Sir George E. Foster, 1929.*

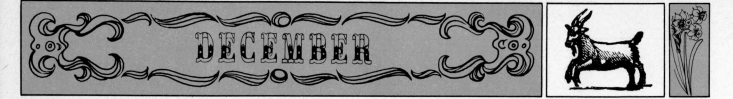
We had no sugar-kettle, but a neighbour promised to lend us his, and to give us twenty-eight troughs, on condition that we gave him half the sugar we made ... I was heartily sick of the sugar-making long before the season was over, however we were well paid for our trouble. Besides one hundred and twelve pounds of fine soft sugar, as good as Muscovado, we had had six gallons of molasses, and a keg containing six gallons of excellent vinegar. There was no lack, this year, of nice preserves, and pickled cucumbers, dainties found in every Canadian establishment.

'Roughing It In The Bush' by Susanna Moodie, 1852.

Rideau Hall, 1868. The Public Archives of Canada

DID YOU KNOW THAT

Proclamation on Vice-Regal Drawing Room.

Ladies to wear low-necked dresses, without COURT TRAINS. Gentlemen in full dress. Ladies, whose health will not admit of their wearing low-necked dresses, may, on forwarding to the A.D.C. in waiting a medical certificate to that effect, wear square-cut dresses.

E. G. P. LITTLETON, Military Secretary to Lord Lorne, Governor General, Montreal, 1878.

Long before tannic acid made itself known, the original prairie women used tea leaves as a remedy for burns. For a bleeding cut, they found that wool, off a sheep's back, was an excellent bandage and cure. Cobwebs, wheat flour and salt in a poultice stopped bleeding. For a sore throat, they applied salt pork cut up small with onions. Onion juice was a sure cure for colds. Poultices of milk and bread, plus fresh vegetable in thin strips and clean wet earth, were applied to insect bites and stings.

The fur-traders in the N.W.T. may have missed the traditional eggnog on New Year's Day but they made up for it in the spring. They found at that season they could use sturgeon roe 'stirred smartly while putting in the rum' with excellent results.

Does anybody in Quebec, or in Saskatchewan for that matter, recall that what is now Saskatchewan was once a portion of Quebec? Hansard will reveal that 'under the Quebec Act of 1774, the western limit of what is now (1875) the province of Quebec was fixed at the forks of the Saskatchewan and the headwaters of the Mississippi.'

As to Ontario – 'By an Order-in-council in 1791, it was declared that the limit of Ontario should extend to what was known as the western limit of Canada under the French, ... the Rocky Mountains.'

A very old cook book of the early 1700's, written by Mrs. Edward Wolfe, mother of Major-General James Wolfe, hero of Quebec, gives this recipe, recommended in England.

'A good water for Consumption'.

Take a peck of green garden snails, wash them in Bear (beer) put them in an oven and let stay till they've done crying; then with a knife and fork prick the green from them, and beat the snail shells and all in a stone mortar. Then take a quart of green earth-worms, slice them through the middle and strow them with salt; then wash them and beat them, the pot being first put into the still with two handfuls of angelico, a quart of rosemary flowers, then the snails and worms, the egrimony, bears feet, red dock roots, barbery brake, bilbony, wormwood, of each two handfuls; one handful of red tumerick and one ounce of saffron, well dried and beaten. Then power (pour) in three gallons of milk. Wait till morning, then put in three ounces of cloves (well beaten), hartshorn, grated. Keep the still covered all night. This done, stir it not. Distil with a moderate fire. The patient must take two spoonfuls at a time.

Before the coming of the white man, the Indians had never heard a cry similar to our lumberjack's 'Timber', nor seen anything like their wood felling methods. For them, clearing land was most difficult. Branches were hacked off the main tree trunk, and piled close round the bottom. Most of this was destroyed by fire. Then the women cleared away what they could, with their rude tools of wood and bone, so that they could plant tobacco, sunflowers, a sort of hemp, beans, corn and pumpkins. Often fish were buried with the seeds as fertilizer. In spite of the primitive customs, the crops did well – something they attributed to the ritual songs and dances at planting time and at harvesting.

To-day on the Gaspé Peninsula, farmers still place fish heads in the earth as they sow.

The well-known hymn 'What a Friend We Have in Jesus' was written by Joseph Medlicott Scriven, at Bewdley, Ontario. His faith survived great personal tragedy. As a young man in Ireland, his bride-to-be, while riding, was thrown from her horse into a stream and drowned just a few hours before the wedding ceremony.

Later, after he came to Canada in 1844, he fell in love with a girl who became a Baptist to please him. When she was immersed, she took a chill which caused her death.

The little cabin where he lived still stands at Bewdley.

'The climate of Manitoba consists of seven months of Arctic winter and five months of cold weather'. – Northern Pacific Railway Co., 'Settler's guide to the North-west', N.Y., 1882.

'Les bottes sauvages', the footgear of the voyageurs, were made without heels for a very definite and practical reason: the heels would destroy their snowshoes, and the men knew that a quick turn to the deep snow was often necessary.

During the 'daft days' (Dec. 24 to 'Auld Handsel', the first Monday of the New Year) old country settlers served tasty 'gudebread' for luck.

A Lacrosse Match on the Ice.
The Public Archives of Canada

OUR GRASS ROOTS

December 30th marks the anniversary of the birth in 1869 of Stephen Leacock, humorist, humanist, teacher, economist and historian. Had this Almanac the power, it would declare a yearly Leacock Day to honour the man who gave the world so much laughter.

To explain the Christmas story of the Three Wise men to the Hurons in the early 1600's, Father Jean de Brébeuf told of chieftains who brought the Infant Child rich furs of beaver, soft moccasins of elk and feather quills of great beauty. The natives responded so well to this tale that Father Brébeuf went on to write them a Christmas hymn.

'When I graduated in England, I couldn't see much use in stalking around Harley Street. Of course, I might have made a lot of money like others, but that wasn't what I wanted. I wanted to do something to help others.'

Dr. Wilfred Grenfell, who went to Labrador in 1892 to establish medical missions.

'My lengthening experience of university work makes me realize more and more that the best parts of a university training and of university life are the by-products of it.'

Stephen Leacock, 1921.

In the famed Malamute Saloon of the Klondike, oldtimers delighted in serving an ice worm cocktail to the cheechakos or greenhorns who were brash enough to call themselves sourdoughs before they had spent a year in the territory and witnessed the spring 'Break-up'. Used only when it seemed that a cheechako was asking for his comeuppance, the ice worms were a specialty carefully prepared and kept in sealed jars. No bartender ever divulged the secret formula.

To down the cocktail with the sourdoughs looking on was a cruel test for the newcomer. He was never told that the little ice worm blinking up through the liquor was an inch of spaghetti, coloured in beet juice with black ink dots for eyes.

Albertans, at this time, relish a special cake called the Pioneer's New Year Celebration Delight.

Happy New Year!
Hogmanay–
Trollolay–
Gie's o' your white bread
And nane o' your grey.

'I went with Madame Baby at five in the morning to the Cathedral Church, to see the illuminations of the altar . . . I was wrapped up very much, and wore a kind of cloth lined with eiderdown, a very comfortable head-dress, but the cold was intense, for the Roman Catholics will not admit of fires in their churches, lest the pictures be spoiled.'
Mrs. John Graves Simcoe in her diary, Quebec, December, 1791.

'The jolting corduroy roads are a disgrace. In Canada, many roads over swamps and gullies are of round logs of wood, or trees, averaging a foot in diameter, laid close by one another and the spaces between unfilled. These turnpikes are fancied to resemble that famous King's cloth, called Corduroy – hence their name.

'In a wagon, the poor human frame is jolted to pieces. Out of evil comes good. Were the country people to take too much care of their roads so that passengers would have no reason to complain, then they would receive no aid from Colonial funds . . . They will gradually improve – for when the officers of State take a drive, or when members of Parliament travel, the Road Bill and Turnpike Act are forced upon their recollections. The Corduroy roads send in their petitions in earnest.'

From a report on 'The Actual State of Canada, 1826, 7, 8' by John Mactaggart, civil engineer, British Government:

'I do not believe that any nation has now attained, and I doubt whether any nation ever will attain, such a point of morality as to govern other nations for the benefit of the governed.'
Goldwin Smith, 1881.

CANADIAN COAT OF ARMS

PROVINCIAL CRESTS

Alberta

British Columbia

Manitoba

New Brunswick

Newfoundland

North West Territories

Nova Scotia

Ontario

Prince Edward Island

Quebec

Saskatchewan

Yukon

PROVINCIAL FLOWERS

Wild Rose
Alberta

Dogwood Flower
British Columbia

Crocus
Manitoba

Purple Violet
New Brunswick

Pitcher Plant
Newfoundland

Mountain Avens
North West Territories

Trailing Arbutus
Nova Scotia

White Trillium
Ontario

Ladyslipper
Prince Edward Island

White Lily
Quebec

Prairie Lily
Saskatchewan

Fireweed
Yukon

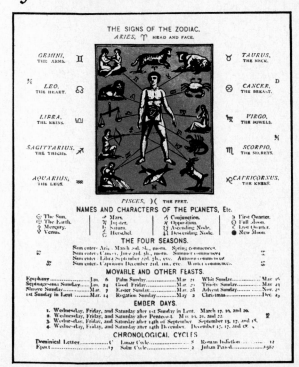

ZODIAC

DAYS OF THE ZODIAC

Aries	March 21-April 19
Taurus	April 20-May 20
Gemini	May 21-June 21
Cancer	June 22-July 22
Leo	July 23-August 22
Virgo	August 23-September 22
Libra	September 23-October 23
Scorpio	October 24-November 22
Sagittarius	November 23-December 21
Capricorn	December 22-January 19
Aquarius	January 20-February 18
Pisces	February 19-March 20